From the moment yo... ...vivid picture of how (... ...captivating journey that wi... ...your desire to discover each new dimension of who you are.

—CARL STEPHENS
PASTOR, FAITH ASSEMBLY
ORLANDO, FLORIDA

One of the greatest challenges in our culture today is identity. We're torn by identity politics, and university classrooms teaching gender, racial, or ethnic identity are packed with students searching for meaning in who they are. Now Mike Shreve has uncovered the roots of our real identity—what God calls us. In his book *Who Am I?* you'll discover exactly who you are from God's perspective, and you'll never look at your life, your purpose, or your destiny the same way again.

—PHIL COOKE
TELEVISION PRODUCER, MEDIA CONSULTANT
AUTHOR, *ONE BIG THING*

I have known Mike Shreve for about thirty years. After coming out of a cult and into the glorious light of God, he has never looked back. Both sinner and saint will reap bountifully from this anointed book—from the abundant scripture in the book plus all of the scripture at the end of each chapter. This book will revolutionize your life when you realize all God has done for us!

—DR. ROBERT D'ANDREA
FOUNDER AND CEO, CHRISTIAN TELEVISION NETWORK

As the family of God, we are about to embark on a glorious new wave of Holy Spirit power. Mike Shreve's book *Who Am I?* provides the scriptural decrees that establish our God-intended identity to receive our rightful inheritance as children of God. Bob and I are thankful for Mike's diligence, passion, and boldness to embrace the richness of God's design that is available to each one of us! We highly endorse this book to help us as believers to awaken to our true spiritual identity—let's effectively prepare our hearts for the manifest presence of God on this earth!

—AUDREY AND BOB MEISNER
TV HOSTS, *MY NEW DAY*
BEST-SELLING AUTHORS, *MARRIAGE UNDERCOVER*

This book and these dynamic declarations will make you normal. Normal as defined by the Bible!

—SID ROTH
HOST, *IT'S SUPERNATURAL!*

I absolutely love books that are based solidly on the true teaching of Scripture rather than on personal opinion or experience. In his book *Who Am I?* Mike Shreve does not disappoint. Carefully identifying scriptural names and terms of God's own people—from cover to cover, Genesis to Revelation—Mike builds the divine basis for identity and purpose for every believer to embrace. Particularly in our broken and tormented generation, when individuals by the millions have been born into families that abused, abandoned, or rejected them, this book will be a powerful tool in God's hand to restore their brokenness and daily forge them into kingdom people, prepared to do exploits!

—DONNA J. SCHAMBACH
EVANGELIST
SCHAMBACH MINISTRIES INTERNATIONAL
WWW.SCHAMBACH.ORG

My friend and brother Mike Shreve has a God-given ability to dig up from the Scriptures pearls and diamonds, which he then causes to shine through his writings. May we all who read these pearls of truth dare to wear them, causing us to become all that the Lord in His great, great love has called us to be!

—JAN WILLEM VAN DER HOEVEN
DIRECTOR, INTERNATIONAL CHRISTIAN ZIONIST CENTER
JERUSALEM, ISRAEL

WHO AM I?

MIKE SHREVE

CHARISMA
HOUSE

Most CHARISMA HOUSE BOOK GROUP products are available at special quantity discounts for bulk purchase for sales promotions, premiums, fund-raising, and educational needs. For details, write Charisma House Book Group, 600 Rinehart Road, Lake Mary, Florida 32746, or telephone (407) 333-0600.

WHO AM I? by Mike Shreve
Published by Charisma House
Charisma Media/Charisma House Book Group
600 Rinehart Road
Lake Mary, Florida 32746
www.charismahouse.com

Author's note: All italics in Scripture quotations reflect the author's emphasis with the exception of quotations from the Complete Jewish Bible (CJB), which italicizes Hebrew terms.

Cover design by Lisa Rae McClure
Design Director: Justin Evans

Visit the author's website at www.shreveministries.org.

Library of Congress Cataloging-in-Publication Data
Names: Shreve, Mike, author.
Title: Who am I? / Mike Shreve.
Description: First edition. | Lake Mary : Charisma House, 2016.
Identifiers: LCCN 2016013906| ISBN 9781629986692 (trade paper)
| ISBN
    9781629986708 (e-book)
Subjects: LCSH: Identity (Psychology)--Religious aspects--
Christianity. |
    Identification (Religion) | God (Christianity)--Love.
Classification: LCC BV4509.5 .S495 2016 | DDC 248.4--dc23
LC record available at http://lccn.loc.gov/2016013906

While the author has made every effort to provide accurate Internet addresses at the time of publication, neither the publisher nor the author assumes any responsibility for errors or for changes that occur after publication.

First edition

16 17 18 19 20 — 987654321
Printed in the United States of America

I dedicate this book to my beloved parents, Andrew and Winnie Shreve, who have new names now, for they overcame and went on to their heavenly reward. They gave me my natural identity "in Adam" that I might live in this world and learn my true spiritual identity "in the Lord."

— — — — — — — — — — — — —

I deeply appreciate all the authors who inspired me in the beginning of my Christian walk with their books on the names and titles of God. As I studied that well-loved, often-taught, foundational biblical revelation, this fresh, God-breathed insight into the names and the titles of the children of God was awakened within my heart. These two related concepts have been eagle's wings to my spirit, carrying me upward to God's "high and holy place" (Isa. 57:15).

CONTENTS

INTRODUCTION

VERY EARLY IN life babies learn to recognize the sound of their names. This awakens within them a sense of security, identity, and belonging. This happens in the natural, but a similar kind of awakening should happen on a spiritual level too.

Early in our walk with God we who are "born again" should learn the wondrous revelation of the many names and titles our heavenly Father has bestowed upon us. This should awaken within us an even greater sense of supernatural security, identity, and belonging.

Where can believers find such a unique and important insight? There is only one reputable source: the Bible.

The word for Bible comes from the Greek word *biblos,* which means "book." So if you call it *"the* Bible," you are actually calling it *"the* Book." There are millions of books in this world, but only one can be called "the Book": the book of all books—the main source of wisdom that human beings need above all others. Interestingly "the Book" is actually a composite of sixty-six books—from Genesis to Revelation—written by about forty authors during a period of approximately 1,500 years.

This Book of books is an amazing tapestry of divinely inspired stories, parables, revelations, commandments, promises, and prophecies that reveal five primary things:

1. Who God is

2. Who we are

3. What the Creator has done and will do for us

4. What we are called to do for Him

5. What our destiny is together (God and His people), both in this world and the world to come

There are certainly other subjects covered in Scripture, but these are the five big ones. Everything else is peripheral.

Though all five are vital issues, our main focus will be numbers two, four, and five: who we are, what we are called to do for God, and what our destiny is together. As we study fifty-two of the most inspiring names and titles God has given His people, it will thrust us into a grand, panoramic view of our spiritual identity, our inheritance in Christ, and the glory of what awaits us in eternity.

By the time you reach the end, you might be heard asking God a question such as, "Who am I that You are so mindful of me, Lord, that You would assign to me such value, such purpose, such authority, and such an amazing future?"

His response might be an echo of an utterance already spoken in ancient times, "Thus says the LORD...I have loved you with an everlasting love; therefore with lovingkindness I have drawn you" (Jer. 31:2–3).

Yes, the high and lofty God truly loves us. He cares for His offspring deeply, and He is drawing us into an identity, an inheritance, and a position in His everlasting kingdom that defies description. Though He has hidden the fullness of its glory from us, from time to time He opens the door slightly to give us a compelling glimpse.

Actually each name and title He gives us is one of those open doors, revealing the heart of the Father toward His beloved. Through the opening His brilliant truth and radiant, divine love shine brightly.

GOD'S HEART TOWARD CREATION

When God created the universe, its immensity and complexity did not prevent Him from being personally involved in the smallest individual parts. Psalm 147:4 even reveals that "He counts the number of the stars; He calls them all by their names."

Selah. Pause for a moment and reflect on the profoundness of that statement. If each one of the billions of stars that fill the cosmos—though inanimate and separate from the Creator—is individually named by the Star maker, then shouldn't we—who are very much alive and filled with God's presence—expect the same treatment?

If God names them, then surely He will name us.

Stars cannot respond to the Most High in reciprocated love. Stars cannot yield to the beauty of His flawless character or reflect His wondrous attributes. Stars cannot return worship to the God who placed them in the heavenly dome, nor can they fill the universe with His praise.

Yet He gives them all names.

If burning spheres of gaseous vapors are that significant to Him, how much more are those who love Him deeply in return, who bear His image, who declare His majesty with uplifted voices.

Maybe for each star, one name was sufficient. But for the sons and daughters of God, hundreds of names are necessary so that He might fully describe who we are and how we fit into His remarkable plan that spans the ages.

What's in a Name?

My wife, Elizabeth, and I considered the choosing of names for offspring a sacred act. We took this responsibility seriously, knowing that the names we selected would mark our offspring for life. Choosing the names of favorite celebrities was never a consideration. Choosing traditional names passed through the family was good but not good enough. Our expectation was that our children's names would guide them prophetically into their destiny.

Our firstborn was a boy. After much prayer, we called him Zion Seth (Zion probably means fortress; Seth means appointed). It was our way of praying that the Almighty would "appoint" him to be a "fortress" of faith in a world filled with doubt, a "fortress" of truth in a world full of deception.

Ten years later Elizabeth became pregnant again. After five months we received a very disturbing report—our daughter, yet in the womb, had spina bifida (a hole in the spine) and would probably have cretinism (mental retardation). Though the doctor knew we were ministers, he had the audacity to suggest abortion as an alternative to carrying the baby full term. We never went back to that physician. Instead, we responded by naming our yet-to-be-born, precious girl Destiny Hope. It was our way of dismissing the negative report by raising a faith-filled banner over her entrance into the world. Yes, it was our way of announcing, *"Little baby, no matter what they say, we declare that you have a destiny and you have hope. The One who formed you in the womb will perfect you, just as Psalm*

138:8 *declares.*" And it happened. Faith attracted the power of God, and our baby girl was born perfect.

So name-giving can be an expression of prophetic intercession—with transformational, even supernatural and miraculous results—especially when God does it.

MY AWAKENING TO THIS REVELATION

Years ago I was involved in an in-depth study of the names and titles given to God in Scripture. It powerfully pulled back the veil on the true nature of the Creator, allowing me to behold the glory of who He is and what I should expect in my relationship with Him.

Incredible confidence was released in me when I came to know Him as my Redeemer, Savior, Sure Foundation, and the Chief Cornerstone of my life! What a blessing it was to discover that He is the Lord my righteousness, the Lord my healer, the Lord my provider, the Lord my shepherd, and the Lord who is always there! What a sense of security I felt upon realizing He is both the Author and the Finisher of my faith (Heb. 12:2)!

I learned in the King James Version of Psalm 91:1 that when I dwell in "the secret place of the most High" (*El Elyon* in Hebrew) then I "abide under the shadow of the Almighty" (*El Shaddai* in Hebrew). In other words, when I make Him the Most High—higher than all my dreams, goals, possessions, and attainments—His mighty power overshadows my life to perform His purpose *marvelously.*

Praise God! My spirit soared. That word study empowered me to rise to the next level spiritually. Nothing I had considered up to that point could compare to this revelatory subject. Then one day—unmistakably, profoundly—the Lord spoke to my heart something that would change my life forever. He communicated *that it would be just as important for me to know my God-given names and titles.*

A spiritual menorah was lit with holy fire deep in my soul.

I began zealously searching the Word. Much to my surprise I found not just dozens but hundreds of names and entitlements. Excitement surged through my spirit. With great gratitude, I realized God had led me to a mother lode, a primary vein of gold in His Word that would enrich me for the rest of my days. More importantly, it would enable me to enrich others. Each title was like another nugget—a shining, golden declaration of who we are in God's great plan of the ages. I felt like a spiritual prospector dancing with glee at the sight of each gleaming, new discovery peeking out of the soil.

Poring over the Scriptures with fresh fervor, my heart was filled again and again with great expectations as I learned what it means for us to be the apple of God's eye, ambassadors for Christ, the bride, children of Abraham, children of the resurrection, a chosen generation, the church, disciples, heirs of the kingdom, heirs of promise, the light of the world, more than conquerors, new creations, overcomers, the redeemed, a royal priesthood, the salt of the earth, true worshippers, vessels of mercy, and much more.

The greatest transformation came not in my knowing but in my doing. It was wonderful to discover and know my identity in God, but it was far more wonderful to actually walk in the reality of that revelation—in tangible and relevant ways. Now it's my blessed privilege and my sacred charge to pass this glorious gift to you.

Because this revelation will prove to you how *loved, blessed, transformed, called, empowered, victorious, and destined* you really are, I have divided all of the names and titles in this book into those seven categories.

I urge you to do more than just accept them by faith. Be filled with wonder. Respond with worship. Then make it happen. Walk in the reality they declare—until you become who you really are. You will never be the same. But more importantly, the world around you will be changed forever as well.

PART 1

- - - - - - - - - -

YOU ARE LOVED

Chapter 1

THE APPLE OF HIS EYE

He who touches you touches the apple of His eye.
—**ZECHARIAH 2:8**

CONTRARY TO POPULAR belief, the phrase "the apple of the eye" has nothing to do with the fruit. Rather, the "apple" is the pupil, the center most part of the eye.

When we refer to someone as the apple of our eye, it is a symbolic, poetic way of saying that person is central to our lives and deeply cherished. How encouraging it is to know God feels this way about His people! We are the center of His attention and the focus of His love. We are the "main event" on the stage of all that He is doing universally.

In this particular verse God is talking about how He feels when we are unjustly persecuted by others. When He says, "He who touches you," He means someone fighting you, withstanding you, or speaking against you in a harmful way. Another version of this same passage has God saying, "Anyone who strikes you strikes what is most precious to me" (Zech. 2:8, GNT).

So in essence God is saying, "If someone mistreats or persecutes any of My offspring, it's as if that person is belligerently jabbing his finger right in the middle of My eye." Surely such a statement is true even when those guilty of mistreating or persecuting God's people are not human, but evil principalities and powers.

Why would the Creator feel this way? Because one of the things that pains God most is the pain of His people. When the Lord Jesus confronted Saul of Tarsus on the road to Damascus, He gave the stern rebuke, "Saul, Saul, why do you persecute Me?" (Acts 9:4). Notice He did not say, "Why do you persecute My people?" but rather, "Why do you persecute Me?" Even though it was actually the believers on earth who were being tortured and martyred, God in heaven related to their suffering as if it was His own.

That same God feels deeply all the pain that you feel as well.

First Appearance in Scripture

The first place in the Bible we find this name for God's people is in "The Song of Moses." (See Deuteronomy 31:30–32:43.) This great prophet was celebrating how God dealt with the nation of Israel soon after they came out of Egypt:

> For the Lord's portion is His people; Jacob is the place of His inheritance. He found him in a desert land and in the waste-land, a howling wilderness; He encircled him, He instructed him, He kept him as *the apple of His eye*.
>
> —Deuteronomy 32:9–10, nkjv

Let's inspect each of the phrases in verse 10 individually.

He encircled him.

Every night of the Israelites' wilderness journey, God surrounded them with warm rays of heavenly light that radiated from the pillar of fire to the outermost edge of the camp. That was the Creator of the universe embracing each one of them as they slept under His stars. Not one was left alone in the darkness. During the hot desert days He was always there, overshadowing them with a cloudy pillar and guiding them to their destination.

He instructed him.

God was constantly training His people during their forty-year trek through the wilderness of sin (and instructing all who would ever learn of this amazing divine intervention as well). He taught them faith when they passed through the Red Sea. He taught them His provisionary care when the manna came down from heaven. He taught them His commandments and the fear of the Lord at Mount Sinai. He taught them the consequence of sin when some resisted His will. He taught them how to be forgiven and to enter His presence when He gave the design for the tabernacle, its priesthood, and its sacrifices. He touched every part of their lives with the Torah (the first five books of the Bible), even prophesying of the Messiah to come. Yes, He schooled them for four decades to prepare them for the Promised Land, for the eventual coming of the new covenant many centuries later and the new creation—His ultimate plan.

He kept him as the apple of His eye.

The Complete Jewish Bible says that Yahweh guarded the seed of Abraham like "the pupil of His eye" (Deut. 32:10). The desert could have easily destroyed the Israelites without divine intervention. There was no water, no food, and intense heat. But God solved all of those problems supernaturally. He even preserved their garments and shoes for forty years. He watched over them to keep them. Most human beings are extremely careful to guard their own eyes, knowing they are an indispensable gift and an irreplaceable treasure. God also watches over His people to guard them, for as far as He is concerned, they are indispensable and irreplaceable. We can expect the same three expressions of divine care from Him as well in this era. He will encircle us, instruct us, and keep us.

THE NEW COVENANT APPLICATION

Deuteronomy 32:10 is lifted to the next level when applied prophetically to the incarnation of the Messiah and the change of the covenant. Remember, God said He would keep Israel as "the apple of His eye."

To understand this word picture we have to ask, "How does one 'keep' or 'guard' his or her eyes?" Simple. The arm is quickly raised to fend off any blow or dangerous object, for any sensible person is far more willing to suffer a temporary bruise to the arm than a permanent injury to the eyes.

In a spiritual sense that's what God did at Calvary. In a manner of speaking, He raised His arm and took the blow. You see, in the ancient days the Promised One was referred to biblically as "the arm of the Lord," as in the following two prophecies of Isaiah:

> The LORD has bared *His holy arm* in the eyes of all the nations, and all the ends of the earth shall see the salvation of our God.
> —ISAIAH 52:10

> Who has believed our report? And to whom has *the arm of the LORD* been revealed?
> —ISAIAH 53:1

When the Son of God was lifted up on the cross, as God's holy arm, He took the deathblow of sin that should have permanently blinded all of us to the things of God, and He did it especially to preserve and protect His cherished ones—all who would ever belong to Him in a covenant relationship—that we might *see* His glory, both now and forevermore.

We owe Him an eternity of praise.

RESPONDING IN GREAT GRATITUDE

When we glimpse God's extravagant love toward us in keeping us from this dangerous world and preserving us in this valley of the shadow of death, it becomes imperative that we respond with gratitude. God discloses the best method of returning His exceptional kindness in Proverbs 7:2:

> Keep My commandments and live, and my teaching as *the apple of your eye.*

In other words, God is saying, "Focus on My Word with passion and devotion. Embrace My commandments. Just as the eyes are the gateway to the soul, let the truth of My Word be the gateway to your heart. Let My promises forever be at the very center of all that you are and all that you do." This is truly the least we can do.

DECLARE WHO YOU ARE IN CHRIST!

> *I declare that I am the apple of God's eye! Therefore, I am the focus of His attention and the gateway to His heart. He cares for me deeply. He watches over me constantly. He guards me every moment. He keeps me. As human beings protect their own eyes, knowing how precious they are, so God protects me, for I am truly precious to Him. I love the Lord Jesus Christ, and He loves me. I can rest secure in these truths all of my days. In Jesus's name, amen!*

Additional reading: Psalms 17:8; 91:11; 121:4–5; 1 Peter 1:3–5

Chapter 2

HIS BELOVED

As He says also in Hosea: "I will call them My people, who were not My people, and her *beloved*, who was not beloved."
—**ROMANS 9:25, NKJV**

HOSEA SPOKE PROPHETICALLY over Israel by means of a strange, yet God-inspired dramatic act. During a time when the nation had plunged into apostasy, he was directed to marry a whorish woman named Gomer (representing the spiritual "whorishness" of Israel at that time). In Hosea chapter 1 we read that Hosea had three children by this woman of stained character: first, Jezreel (a son), then Lo-Ruhamah (a daughter), then Lo-Ammi (another son). Their names were intentional prophetic statements declaring the serious consequences that would soon befall the northern kingdom of Israel because of their idolatry and their blatant disregard for the covenant they had with the true God.

+ **Jezreel** means God sows, and signifies scattering, as in the scattering of seed—for they were soon to be strewn like seed throughout the world.[1]

+ **Lo-Ruhamah** means not having obtained mercy—for God was no longer going to pour out patience and pity on them.

+ **Lo-Ammi** means not My people—for God was saying, "We are no longer in a special relationship; you no longer belong to Me."

Soon after these acted-out-prophecies, the Israelites were crushed by the Assyrian army and carried away into captivity. Thankfully, in the midst of such grievous darkness, a bright light shone forth, for Hosea proclaimed the coming of a glorious future day when the children of Israel (the northern kingdom of ten tribes) and the children of Judah (the southern kingdom of two tribes) would be reunited under one head (Hos. 1:11).

That ancient prophecy was fulfilled when the Messiah came but in far greater measure than they expected, for He conquered the grave and ascended to heaven in order to become the head, not only of Israel and Judah but also of all the Gentiles who would place their trust in Him (Eph. 1:22). In this new covenant era all people of all races and tongues who repent and believe are "married...to Him who has been raised from the dead" (Rom. 7:4)—becoming a part of His eternal bride. As the Apostle Paul wrote, "The husband is the head of the wife, just as Christ is the head and Savior of the church" (Eph. 5:23).

God revealed the beauty of this era through Hosea's words, especially in the following three verses:

+ "And it shall be, in that day," says the LORD, "That you will call Me 'My Husband,' and no longer call Me 'My Master'" (Hosea 2:16, NKJV).

+ "I will betroth you to Me forever; yes, I will betroth you to Me in righteousness and justice, in lovingkindness and mercy" (Hosea 2:19, NKJV).

+ "Then...I will have mercy on her who had not obtained mercy; then I will say to those who were not My people, 'You are My people!' And they shall say, 'You are my God!'" (Hosea 2:23, NKJV).

About eight centuries later Paul referred to this last verse in his epistle to the Romans, yet enhanced its meaning with additional wording:

> As He says also in Hosea: "I will call them My people, who were not My people; and her *beloved*, who was not beloved. And it shall come to pass in the place where it was said to them, 'You are not My people,' there they shall be called sons of the living God."
>
> —ROMANS 9:25–26, NKJV

Far in advance, therefore, God planned a miraculous reconciliation and a major spiritual shift, both for the Israelite people who had fallen away and the Gentiles who had never been included. The future offspring of those groups of people estranged from Him under the old covenant would be given the opportunity, under the new covenant, to enter a deep, full, and loving relationship with the Father of creation.

Instead of being rejected by God, we who respond are now "accepted in the Beloved" (Eph. 1:6, NKJV). Because of our union with the Lord Jesus, we are just as welcome in the presence of the Father as the firstborn Son—for "through Him [Jesus] we both have access by one Spirit to the Father" (Eph. 2:18; see also Matthew 3:17).

Jesus actually prayed we would be established in this covenant of love in His great intercessory prayer over the church:

> Father…I have given them the glory which You gave Me, that they may be one even as We are one: I in them and You in Me, that they may be perfect in unity, and that the world may know that You have sent Me, and *have loved them as You have loved Me.*
>
> —JOHN 17:1, 22–23

What an amazing revelation! Jesus wanted "the world" to know that both He and His bride (the church) are equally beloved of the Father—that the same depth of infinite love bestowed on Him has been bestowed on us. Unfortunately many believers have never seen this breathtaking view of who we are in God's great plan.

No wonder Paul said the love of Christ "surpasses knowledge" (Eph. 3:19). It cannot be comprehended intellectually; it must be experienced. Though we were once "far away," we have now been "brought near by the blood of Christ" (Eph. 2:13). Though many of us can look back in regret to a "Gomer-like" past, we are now "the dearly beloved" of His soul for time and eternity (Jer. 12:7).

By the way, the names have changed for God's chosen people under the new covenant. We are now called Ammi, meaning "My people," and Ruhamah, meaning those who have "obtained mercy"[2] (Hosea 2:1). Furthermore, in a positive sense we have become "Jezreel" ("the seed of God"[3] sown in the earth) and as the prophet said, "Great will be the day of Jezreel" (Hosea 1:11).

Our hearts should overflow with gratitude even now.

Declare Who You Are in Christ!

I declare that I am in the beloved! I am a part of the bride of Christ, just as beloved of the Father as Jesus, the firstborn Son, and just as accepted in His presence. I declare that nothing can separate me from this divine love and that by it, I am more than a conqueror in everything I face in this world. I am not separated from God anymore; I am part of a group He calls "Ammi," "Ruhamah," and "Jezreel." We are His people. We have obtained mercy. We are the seed of God sown in the earth and great will be our day! We will bring forth a harvest in the earth for His glory and celebrate His great love for us by sharing that love with others every day. In Jesus's name, amen!

Additional reading: Psalm 108:5–6; Romans 5:5; Ephesians 1:4; 3:14–21; 1 John 4:7–9; 16–18

Chapter 3

THE BRIDE

One of the seven angels...said to me, "Come, I
will show you *the bride*, the wife of the Lamb."
—**REVELATION 21:9**

AFTER THE ANGEL invited John to behold the Lord's "bride," a stunning vision unfolded before him.

> And he carried me away in the Spirit to a great and high mountain, and showed me the Holy City, Jerusalem, descending out of heaven from God, having the glory of God, her light like a most precious jewel, like a jasper, clear as crystal.
> —REVELATION 21:10–11

What a strange revelation! The angel told John he would see a bride and instead he saw a city—but it wasn't just any city. It was "New Jerusalem," the capital city of the new creation, "prepared as a bride adorned for her husband" (Rev. 21:2).

Of course, it's not so much the city but the inhabitants of that city who will be married to the heavenly Bridegroom. However, the city and the bride are one. Because of this, certain details about the city supply symbolic and prophetic statements about the nature of those "lovers of God" who will be rapturously and infinitely joined in a spiritual, marital union to the Lord of creation.

THE GATES AND THE FOUNDATIONS

For hundreds of years students of the Word have pondered the mystery of who constitutes "the bride." Is it comprised of the whole body of Christ or just those who walk in intimacy with the Lord? Is it made up of just new covenant saints or are old covenant Israelites included? Symbolism is the language of God, and through the symbolism of Revelation 2:12 and 14, God gives the simple answer. In describing the eternal city, John said:

> She had a great and high wall with twelve gates, and twelve angels at the gates, and names written on them, which are the names of *the twelve tribes of the children of Israel.*
> —REVELATION 21:12, NKJV

> The wall of the city had twelve foundations, and on them were the names of *the twelve apostles of the Lamb.*
> —REVELATION 21:14

So the twelve gates are named after the twelve tribes of Israel (God's people under the old covenant), and the twelve foundations are named after the twelve apostles of the Lamb (those used of God to usher in the new covenant). This indicates that there is a mixture of both covenants in the city of God. All its citizenry enter the city through the gates of the law (that revelation from the old covenant that reveals our guiltiness in the sight of God), but are established on the foundation of that grace that came through the new covenant (by the crucifixion and resurrection of the Son of God). All the redeemed of both covenants are married to God eternally and will ever be a part of His bridal company.

THE GATES OF PEARLS

> The twelve gates were twelve pearls, each of the gates made of a single pearl.
> —REVELATION 21:21

Pearls are produced when a parasite or a grain of sand becomes lodged in the folds of an oyster's flesh. Unable to rid itself of this "uninvited guest," the oyster will secrete a milk-like substance called nacre and coat the "intruder" over and over until finally something valuable and beautiful is created out of that which initially seemed only worthless and painful. And so it is with our lives. We learn to respond to all the negative things we face in this world by covering them—over and over again—with the "milk" of God's Word (1 Pet. 2:2). This process will teach us lessons here in this world that are valuable and beautiful and will ultimately become a gate to an eternal heavenly dwelling place.

THE GOLD

And the city was pure gold, as clear as glass.

—REVELATION 21:18

Because it is one of the most valuable metals, gold is a fitting biblical symbol of the divine nature. During his great trial Job said, "I will come forth as gold" (Job 23:10). In other words, he knew God would use all of his adversities to mature him spiritually and to advance him in godlike character. He knew he would be better off in the end than he was in the beginning. When gold is heated and liquefied, the dross floats to the surface so the goldsmith can scoop it away.

So it is for the bride. We may face fiery trials in life, but it is so "the genuineness of your faith, which is more precious than gold that perishes, though it is tried by fire, may be found to result in praise, glory, and honor at the revelation of Jesus Christ" (1 Pet. 1:7).

THE NAME

The name of the eternal city of God is "New Jerusalem." Because *Jerusalem* means possession of peace, *New Jerusalem* implies a new depth of peace far beyond anything we have ever experienced.[1] This was foretold in the beloved prophecy Isaiah gave concerning the coming Messiah:

> For unto us a child is born, unto us a son is given, and the government shall be upon his shoulder. And his name shall be called Wonderful Counselor, Mighty God, Eternal Father, Prince of Peace. Of the increase of his government and peace there shall be no end.
>
> —ISAIAH 9:6–7

After passing through this world with all of its danger, stress, confusion, and strife, the bride will finally possess undisturbed "peace of God, which surpasses all understanding" (Phil. 4:7). God has promised of old, "I will extend peace to her like a river" (Isa. 66:12). Being inundated in His ever-increasing peace will surely be a most excellent gift given to those beloved ones who enjoy a greater intimacy with the Maker of all things than words can describe. Just knowing that the Creator of the universe is in love with us to this degree should warm our hearts beyond description even now.

DECLARE WHO YOU ARE IN CHRIST!

I declare that I belong to the bride of Christ! My heavenly Father has given me the supreme privilege of being "married…to Him who has been raised from the dead" that I might "bear fruit for God" (Rom. 7:4). Because I am the Lamb's wife, I can expect spiritual intimacy with the Lord Jesus. He romances me daily. He would rather spend time with those of us who make up His bride than the most famous, wealthy, intellectual, or influential people in this world who do not know Him. Yes, I declare, the Most High God is in love with me and I am in love with Him. This is a holy union that will never end, and nothing—absolutely nothing—will ever separate me from His great love. In Jesus's name, amen!

Additional reading: Isaiah 62:1–7; Jeremiah 3:14; Romans 8:35–39; Ephesians 5:22–32; Revelation 19:6–9, 21:1–7

Chapter 4

CHILDREN OF PROMISE

Now we, brothers, like Isaac, are the children of promise.
—**GALATIANS 4:28**

A PROMISE IS a pledge, a firm and unwavering agreement; it is a trustworthy announcement that one will or will not do something specified.

God's Word is so filled with promises that Solomon described it in a singular sense as "His good promise" (1 Kings 8:56, NKJV). Of course, Solomon was referring only to those books of the Bible that were recognized as sacred and inspired in his day. Yet this statement could surely be expanded in our day to mean all sixty-six "God-breathed" books of the Bible. From Genesis to Revelation, this holy text truly is "His good promise." It is:

+ The *Word* of God—made up of many inspired words
+ The *Promise* of God—made up of many glorious promises

If the promises of God were removed from the Bible, no one would want to study its content. A promise-less Bible would only serve to decry our dark and dreadful condition as fallen human beings and forewarn the utter bleakness and emptiness of our future.

Ephesians 2:12 describes the multitudes of Gentiles (non-Jews) populating this planet as "strangers to the covenants of promise, without hope and without God in the world."

This was the condition of most of the human race until the Messiah came "to perform the mercy promised" to the forefathers of Israel (Luke 1:72). Though God moved mightily in the former era and introduced many powerful promises under the old covenant, when the King of righteousness walked in this world, He introduced a "better covenant...established on better promises" (Heb. 8:6).

THE NEW APPROACH

Through Jeremiah, God revealed some of the "better promises" that would be available under the coming "new covenant." He foretold:

> Surely, the days are coming, says the LORD, when I will make a new covenant with the house of Israel and with the house of Judah....I will put My law within them and write it in their hearts; and I will be their God, and they shall be My people. They shall teach no more every man his neighbor and every man his brother, saying, "Know the LORD," for they all shall know Me, from the least of them to the greatest of them, says the LORD, for I will forgive their iniquity, and I will remember their sin no more.
>
> —JEREMIAH 31:31, 33–34

Those who desire to enter this new covenant often start by claiming the promises found in Romans 10:9–10:

> If you confess with your mouth Jesus is Lord, and believe in your heart that God has raised Him from the dead, you will be saved, for with the heart one believes unto righteousness, and with the mouth confession is made unto salvation.

When we receive salvation, we are also sealed "with the Holy Spirit of promise, who is the guarantee of our inheritance, until the redemption of the purchased possession" (Eph. 1:13–14, NKJV). In other words, God makes a commitment—He promises—to protect us and preserve us until the day of the resurrection and the completion of His work in us. We can walk in confidence knowing that our Savior is "the author and finisher of our faith" (Heb. 12:2) and that "all the promises of God in Him are 'Yes,' and in Him 'Amen,' to the glory of God through us" (2 Cor. 1:20).

CLAIMING ALL OF GOD'S PROMISES

If just two verses containing two promises (Rom. 10:9–10) could transform us so dramatically (saving us and granting us righteousness), what could happen if our hearts widened to embrace all the pledges God has made to His people? One excellent source claims there are exactly 7,487 promises in God's Word.[1]

Here's a sampling of some of the most important ones:

- Forgiveness and cleansing: "If we confess our sins, He is faithful and just to forgive us our sins and cleanse us from all unrighteousness" (1 John 1:9).

- Peace and protection: "And the peace of God, which surpasses all understanding, will protect your hearts and minds through Christ Jesus" (Phil. 4:7).

- Joy: "Therefore with joy you shall draw water out of the wells of salvation" (Isa. 12:3).

- Love and the Holy Spirit: "And hope does not disappoint, because the love of God is shed abroad in our hearts by the Holy Spirit who has been given to us" (Rom. 5:5).

- Authority and invincibility: "I give you the authority...over all the power of the enemy. And nothing shall by any means hurt you" (Luke 10:19).

- Health: "Who Himself bore our sins in His own body on the tree, that we, having died to sins, might live for righteousness—by whose stripes you were healed" (1 Pet. 2:24, NKJV).

- A sound mind: "For God has not given us a spirit of fear, but of power and of love and of a sound mind" (2 Tim. 1:7, NKJV).

- The kingdom of God: "Listen, my beloved brothers. Has God not chosen the poor of this world to be rich in faith and heirs of the kingdom which He has promised to those who love Him?" (James 2:5).

- Eternal life: "And this is the promise that He has promised us—eternal life" (1 John 2:25).

There is absolutely no problem or challenge you could face in this world that God has not already, in advance, given a promise strong and powerful enough to carry you through to total victory. As 1 John 5:4 states, "For whoever is born of God overcomes the world, and the victory that overcomes the world is our faith." By the way, that verse contains two more promises.

To see these and all other promises come to pass, we should take the following four steps:

1. Embrace the promise.
2. Believe the promise.
3. Confess the promise.
4. Apply the promise to specific circumstances.

After we do these four things, we should then expect the manifestation of the promise in our lives.

Of course, not only do the promises of God deal with the here and now, they also reveal the future, such as the following grand passage:

> The Lord is not slack *concerning His promise*, as some count slackness, but is longsuffering toward us, not willing that any should perish but that all should come to repentance. But the day of the Lord will come as a thief in the night, in which the heavens will pass away with a great noise, and the elements will melt with fervent heat....Nevertheless we, *according to His promise*, look for new heavens and a new earth in which righteousness dwells.
>
> —2 Peter 3:9–10, 13, nkjv

If God promised these things, surely they will come to pass!

Declare Who You Are in Christ

I declare that I am a child of promise and an heir of promise! All 7,487 promises in God's Word belong to me, and I expect them to come to pass in my life. I refuse to be spiritually weak, for I can do all things through Christ who strengthens me. I refuse to be depressed, for the joy of the Lord is my strength. I refuse to be sick, for with His stripes I was healed. I refuse to be bound, because God's Spirit lives in my heart and where the Spirit of the Lord is there is liberty. I refuse to fear death, for I have the promise of eternal life. Yes, I am victorious in all things. In Jesus's name, amen!

Additional reading: Jeremiah 33:14; Acts 1:1–5; Romans 4:13–20; 9:8; Ephesians 6:2; Titus 1:1–2

Chapter 5

GOD'S GARDEN

*We are only God's coworkers. You are God's garden,
not ours; you are God's building, not ours.*
—1 Corinthians 3:9, tlb

A GARDEN IS a haven of rest, a sanctuary of solace, a place of peaceful beauty in a world that is often stressful, painful, and disappointing. For those who feel numb and lifeless from an overload of mundane responsibilities, a garden can be an atmosphere of fresh inspiration and creativity spurred by the delightful fragrances, the symmetry of plant shapes, and the complementary contrasts in color.

Because every expertly planted garden is reminiscent of Eden, it can almost become a portal into the celestial world, at least for those in covenant with the Master Gardener Himself, the One who "planted a garden in the east, in Eden" at the very start (Gen. 2:8).

On the simplest and purist level a garden speaks of love:

- The love of the gardener for His work of art, who envisions a miraculous awakening of potential with each seed that is planted
- The love of the earth, soaking in water and absorbing light, then joyously giving birth to magnificent patterns and hues
- The love that flows from the hearts of those who often visit this near-heavenly refuge from the ravages of time

Yes, a garden truly speaks of love—the love of the Father toward us, our love returning to Him, and the love we should feel for the gift of life and for fellow pilgrims on this journey through time.

A Garden for God

The Song of Songs (also known as the Song of Solomon) is probably the most mysterious and poetically beautiful book of the Bible. It involves a series of complementary exchanges between a shepherd-king-bridegroom and his espoused bride. Full of rich symbolism, it speaks prophetically of the divine romance between the heavenly Shepherd-King-Bridegroom (the Lord Jesus) and His earthborn bride (everyone who has entered into a covenant relationship with Him).

About midway through the story, the Bridegroom woos His bride-to-be with a choice description of her attractiveness:

> A garden enclosed is my sister, my spouse, a spring shut up, a fountain sealed. Your plants are an orchard of pomegranates with pleasant fruits…a fountain of gardens, a well of living waters.
> —Song of Solomon 4:12–15, nkjv

Not only is the bride depicted as a garden in this verse, she is also portrayed as a "fountain of gardens"—because the entire bride of Christ makes up one eternal garden, yet every individual member of the bride is a complete garden as well.

The espoused bride responds by inviting the Shepherd-King to draw near:

> Let my beloved come to his garden and eat its pleasant fruits.
> —Song of Solomon 4:16, nkjv

What are the "pleasant fruits" the bride bids the Bridegroom to ingest when He visits the garden-like souls of those who love Him?

The fruit of the divine nature

The bride produces fruit of the Spirit, including love, joy, and peace—loving the Lord back with the love He has given us, rejoicing before Him with the joy He has given us, and peacefully placing trust in the One who has given peace to us. (See Galatians 5:22–23.) He partakes happily of this fruit, though it came from Him in the first place.

The fruit of souls won in His name

Jesus urged His followers, "Listen! I say to you, lift up your eyes and look at the fields, for they are already white for harvest. He who reaps receives wages, and gathers fruit that leads to eternal life, that both he who sows and he who reaps may rejoice together" (John 4:35–36). When we, the bride of the Lamb, win people to the Lord, we offer them to Him as the fruit of our labor.

The fruit of praise

We also offer the fruit of anointed worship—"Let us continually offer to God the sacrifice of praise, which is the fruit of our lips, giving thanks to His name" (Heb. 13:15).

> For as the earth brings forth her buds, and as the garden causes the things that are sown in it to spring forth, so the Lord God will cause righteousness and praise to spring forth before all the nations.
> —Isaiah 61:11

A Garden to Others

Part of our garden calling is to be a refuge to the hurting and damaged people of this world. Our role is not to be critics and judges. Our purpose is not to bring people into more religious bondage. Rather, we are called to be repairers and restorers. Here is a great passage prophesying this truth:

> If you take away the yoke from your midst, the pointing of the finger, and speaking wickedness, and if you give yourself to the hungry and satisfy the afflicted soul, then your light shall rise in obscurity, and your darkness shall become as the noonday. And the Lord shall guide you continually, and satisfy your soul in drought, and strengthen your bones; and *you shall be like a watered garden, and like a spring of water, whose waters do not fail.* Those from among you shall rebuild the old waste places; you shall raise up the foundations of many generations; and you shall be called, the Repairer of the Breach, the Restorer of Paths in which to Dwell.
> —Isaiah 58:9–12

We are made like a watered garden when our focus is on helping others. A garden does not exist for itself. It exists for the benefit of others. The same is true of us. Thus the very means of becoming a "garden" ends up being the result as well—that is, that others find solace and peace when they're around us and partake of our fruit.

A Garden for Ourselves and for the Gardener

In the kingdom to come, after this earthly pilgrimage is over, the Bridegroom and the bride will dwell together forever in rapturous love. In that day God will certainly give us "beauty for ashes, the oil of joy for mourning" and "the garment of praise for the spirit of heaviness" (Isa. 61:3). We will blossom fully in the things of God and realize the enormity of what He has done for us.

The bride of Christ will finally be a garden for herself (corporately) for there will be no hurting people to minister to. So each member of the bride will find in every other member a refuge of everlasting peace and joy from the painful things we faced during this earthly sojourn. Most importantly we will be a garden for the Bridegroom forevermore. The following two scriptures are a great way of closing the revelation of this chapter:

> For the LORD shall comfort Zion, He will comfort all her waste places; He will make her wilderness like Eden, *and her desert like the garden of the LORD*; joy and gladness shall be found in it, thanksgiving, and the voice of melody.
>
> —ISAIAH 51:3

> For the LORD has redeemed Jacob and ransomed him from the hand of him who was stronger than he. Therefore they will come and sing in the height of Zion, and will be joyful over the goodness of the LORD, for wheat and for wine and for oil and for the young of the flock and of the herd; and *their souls will be as a watered garden*. And they will not sorrow any more at all.
>
> —JEREMIAH 31:11–12

DECLARE WHO YOU ARE IN CHRIST!

I declare that I am part of God's garden! I am also an individual garden that He can visit. As Adam and Eve walked with God in the Garden of Eden, so I invite the Master Gardener to walk with me in the garden of my heart. My highest priority is to produce much fruit for His glory. I invite the Shepherd-King-Bridegroom into my soul to smell the fragrance of my praise and eat the fruit of the Spirit—the character of God—that is being developed in my life. I also desire to be a garden for the destitute and desperate people of this world, so that they can come to me and partake of the fruit of the Spirit in my life. In Jesus's name, amen!

Additional reading: Numbers 24:5–6; Song of Songs 4:1–5:1; 6:1–3; Isaiah 5:7 (NLT)

Chapter 6

HEIRS OF THE GRACE OF LIFE

Likewise, you husbands, live considerately with your
wives, giving honor to the woman as the weaker
vessel, since they too are also *heirs of the grace of
life*, so that your prayers will not be hindered.
—1 Peter 3:7

O F ALL THE titles for God's people that express His great
love for us, this is one of the most excellent. The outpouring of grace is a wondrous gift we have all received as children of the Most High. Be assured, the ground is level at the cross. We were all equally helpless and hopeless until the "God of all grace" condescended to visit us in our low estate (1 Pet. 5:10).

One of my favorite definitions of *grace* is "the divine influence upon the heart and its reflection in the life."[1]

This subliminal, supernatural influence first flows into our hearts to change us. Then it flows out of us to change others. So whenever grace manifests, it always brings change. Such a mysterious, spiritual impartation can be identified four primary ways:

+ Unmerited love from God
+ Imparted ability from God
+ God's abundant generosity toward His people
+ The sum total of all God's activity in our lives

One of the most beautiful revelations of this heaven-sent gift is shared in 2 Corinthians 8:9: "For you know the grace of our Lord Jesus Christ, that though He was rich, yet for your sakes He became poor, that through His poverty you might be rich."

Rich? Jesus? For some that may be hard to imagine. However, this verse is not talking about earthly, temporal riches. The Son of God was "rich" in that which is celestial and eternal. He was rich in the abundance of heaven. He was rich in undisturbed fellowship with the Father. He was rich in the adoration of multitudes of angels. He was rich in the overflow of infinite peace, joy, and love. He was richly clothed in the splendor of paradise. But He divested Himself of His radiant, majestic "garments" to assume the poverty-stricken form of humanity.

When He went to Calvary, He became as poor as anyone can become, for the one thing that did enrich Him—the presence of the Holy Spirit—apparently departed from Him when His soul became an "offering for sin" on the cross (Isa. 53:10). He even cried, "My God, My God, why have You forsaken Me?" (Matt. 27:46).

If we connect with the Lord Jesus at this, His poorest point, He graciously responds by pouring the wealth of heaven into our bankrupt lives. He heaps on us the riches of His goodness, the riches of His mercy, and the riches of His glory. (See Romans 2:4; 9:23; Ephesians 2:4.) Yes, because of His poverty we who were spiritual paupers are made "rich in faith" (James 2:5) and heirs of "the incomprehensible riches of Christ" (Eph. 3:8; see also 1 Samuel 2:7–8).

The One who was most deserving took the place of the least deserving, then shared with them the best of all that He is and all that He has—and all because of His great love.

Yes, beholding and understanding the mystery of this pivotal event in the history of our planet is how we know the grace of God.

ATTITUDES THAT ATTRACT GRACE

Grace is free, absolutely free. It is a gift from above. However, there are three complementary attitudes that place us in a receptive position. Those heart attitudes are faith, humility, and sincere love for God. Here are three scriptures that open up this treasury of divine bounty to us:

> For by grace you have been saved through *faith*, and that not of yourselves; it is the gift of God, not of works, lest anyone should boast.
> —EPHESIANS 2:8–9, NKJV

> God resists the proud, but gives grace to the *humble*.
> —1 PETER 5:5

> Grace be with all those who *love our Lord Jesus Christ in sincerity.* Amen.
>
> —Ephesians 6:24

These three spiritual traits, working together, secure the initial entrance of grace into our lives and ensure its unceasing flow—through all the ups and downs of life. If we maintain these three spiritual attitudes, God promises that He is "able to make *all grace* abound toward you, that you, always having all sufficiency in all things, may have an abundance for every good work" (2 Cor. 9:8, nkjv).

If God is able to make all grace abound toward us that begs the question, "How much grace is 'all' grace?" Surely, it's just as immeasurable and inexhaustible as the One who gives it—but only for those whose hearts are true. It's an infinitely unending river, flowing from the gracious Lord who sits on a "throne of grace" in the heavenly realm. Those who sincerely love Him are invited to come boldly to this throne where they can always find "grace to help in time of need" (Heb. 4:16).

A Wonderful Conclusion

Before you start desperately asking God for more grace in your life, consider the truth that God has "saved us and called us with a holy calling, not by our works, but by His own purpose and grace, which was given us in Christ Jesus before the world began" (2 Tim. 1:9).

Did your mind start expanding as you read that statement? The Most High gave you grace in Christ before time began, before there was an earth rotating on its axis or a swirling Milky Way galaxy spinning in space. Do you think He might have missed His calculations and accidentally foreordained less grace than what you will need to fulfill your purpose? Or did the omniscient, all-knowing God get it right? I believe He anticipated every low valley you will ever walk through—every hurt, every failure, every challenge, and every purpose you will ever be called to fulfill. And in advance He gave you not just enough but *more than enough* grace to recover from the negatives and to attain all the positives.

So maybe, just maybe, you should never ask Him for grace. Instead, you should thank Him that because you belong to Him, and because you are born again, you have already been given more than enough grace to emerge from this life "more than conquerors through Him who loved us" (Rom. 8:37).

Notice in this scripture the word *loved* is in the past tense. He figured this all out before you got here. He loved you even before you existed. So grace really is the conclusion of the whole matter. No wonder the last verse of the Bible declares: "The grace of our Lord Jesus Christ be with you all. Amen" (Rev. 22:21).

DECLARE WHO YOU ARE IN CHRIST!

I declare that I am an heir of the grace of life! I am in covenant with the God of all grace. Right now I approach His throne of grace boldly, expecting to find grace to help in the time of need. I sincerely love God, I humble myself before Him, and I believe utterly in His Word. Because of these three attitudes in my heart toward Him, I am sure God will make all grace abound toward me. Therefore, I will have all sufficiency in all things. God gave me grace in Christ before the world began, so I praise Him for its manifestation in the present. This is my God-given inheritance, and I lay hold to it. In Jesus's name, amen!

Additional reading: Genesis 6:8; Exodus 33:11–18 (NKJV); Zechariah 12:10 (NKJV); Romans 6:14; 1 Corinthians 15:10

Chapter 7

A SPECIAL TREASURE

Now therefore, if you will indeed obey My voice and
keep My covenant, then you shall be *a special treasure*
to Me above all people; for all the earth is Mine.
—Exodus 19:5, nkjv

I AM IN awe—almost unable to write—as I ponder the profound truth of this verse. The Creator of this vast universe says we are a treasure to Him. Although we have all been born in sin and have walked in darkness to one degree or another, the Maker of heaven and earth cherishes us deeply, focuses on us intensely, and values us eternally. This is almost impossible to grasp. Yet it is true.

But there is more. We are not only His treasure; we are also His "special treasure." So of all the things God treasures about creation, evidently the bride of Christ occupies the highest place of esteem. That's not just a divine emotion extended toward the whole family of God—that's how God feels about you, individually and uniquely. You personally are His "special treasure." Isn't that wonderful to know?

When the Son of God walked the earth, He taught His people, "Where your treasure is, there will your heart be also" (Matt. 6:21). If that is true with respect to us, it is also true with respect to God. Where God's treasure is, there will His heart be also. So if you want to know where God's heart is, find His people—because His heart is constantly beating toward every yielded and obedient son or daughter in His family.

THE TREASURE PARABLE

Matthew 13 contains eight parables of the kingdom of heaven and each one unveils significant kingdom mysteries. The fifth parable relates to this chapter's theme:

> Again, the kingdom of heaven is like *treasure hidden in a field*, which a man found and hid. And with joy over it he goes and sells all that he has and buys that field.
>
> —MATTHEW 13:44

+ The man is the Son of man, the Lord Jesus Christ.

+ The treasure is described as hidden in the field because many children of God are "hidden" for a season in a lost lifestyle, and as such they are covered over with the dirt of carnality, sensuality, intellectuality, religiosity, self-centeredness, or rebellion against God.

+ The treasure, once found, is hidden again by its new owner to guard it. When the Son of man found us in our sins, He first cleansed us. Then He hid us "in the shadow of His hand" (Isa. 49:2) and in "the secret place of His tabernacle" (Ps. 27:5, NKJV). Yes, we are now "hidden with Christ in God"—a place of protection and security (Col. 3:3).

+ It is not out of obligation or a sense of duty but for "joy" that the "man" in the parable paid such a sacrificial price to buy that field—for he recognized the value of the treasure. So it is God's joy to save us. (See Jeremiah 33:8–9.) One day He will present us "faultless before the presence of His glory *with exceeding joy*" (Jude 1:24, NKJV).

+ From another parable, we discover that "the field is the world" (Matt. 13:38). So not only did Jesus purchase a redeemed people, He also purchased the whole earth with His sacrifice on Calvary to give it to His bride-elect as an inheritance forever. We, His special treasure, will rule and reign with Him here in a restored paradise world.

DECLARE WHO YOU ARE IN CHRIST!

I declare that I am a special treasure to God. I believe that His heart is inclined toward me every moment of every day. His thoughts toward me are more numerous than the sand of the sea. In great gratitude I make a commitment to always, to the best of my ability, obey His voice and keep

His covenant. I confess that I am hidden in the shadow of God's hand and hidden in the secret of His tabernacle. Because He treasures my relationship with Him, He will guard and protect me all my days. In Jesus's name, amen!

Additional reading: Deuteronomy 26:17–19; Psalm 135:1–4; Titus 2:14

PART 2

- - - - - - - - - - -

YOU ARE BLESSED

Chapter 8

THE BLESSED OF THE FATHER

Then the King will say to those at His right hand,
"Come, you *blessed of My Father*, inherit the kingdom
prepared for you since the foundation of the world."
—MATTHEW 25:34

THE WORD BLESSED means supremely happy, enriched with benefits, spiritually prosperous, and highly favored of God. It also describes someone with character traits God considers to be the highest expression of good, such as meekness, hunger for righteousness, mercifulness, or purity of heart.

In the Bible certain Hebrew and Greek words translated "blessed" are also translated "happy," because blessedness and happiness simply go together.

Such was the spiritual atmosphere of this world at its onset. After creating the creatures of the sky and sea, "then God *blessed* them, saying, 'Be fruitful and multiply'" (Gen. 1:22). After creating Adam and Eve, "then God *blessed* them, and said to them, 'Be fruitful and multiply; fill the earth and subdue it; have dominion'" (Gen. 1:28, NKJV).

From the start the blessing of God was released by the spoken word (it often works that way through us as well). However, after Adam and Eve transgressed, God introduced the curse. (See Genesis 3:14–19.) Since that day every human being has entered this world conceived in iniquity, born in sin, spiritually stained, separated from the Creator, and stalked by death. (See Psalm 51:5; Romans 5:12.) Nevertheless, from the beginning God's intention was to bring forth redemption and restoration by a slowly evolving plan.

The human race arrived at a spiritual milestone centuries later when, after the flood, "God blessed Noah and his sons" (Gen. 9:1). Then ten generations later God revealed Himself to a man named Abraham saying, "I will bless you and make your name great; so that you will be a blessing...and in you all families of the earth will be blessed" (Gen. 12:2–3, ESV).

By obeying God's call, Abraham became the catalyst for the release of God's blessing into all the world. When his descendants entered the land of promise centuries later, thousands of them stood on the slopes of two mountains (Ebal and Gerizim) shouting "amen" to the curses listed in Deuteronomy 27:11–26 and the blessings listed in Deuteronomy 28:1–13. God promised if the Israelites were obedient, those blessings would "overtake" them, ultimately positioning them as "the head" among all nations. Unfortunately such an exalted status hinged on strict adherence to the 613 commandments of the law, the Torah. (See Deuteronomy 27:26.) This former model failed because it depended too much on human performance.

THEN THE MESSIAH CAME

Though the Old Testament ended with the word *curse*, Jesus's first main sermon in the New Testament began with eight statements of blessedness. The first one was:

> Blessed are the poor in spirit, for theirs is the kingdom of heaven.
>
> —MATTHEW 5:3

In other words, *supremely happy, enriched with benefits, spiritually prosperous,* and *highly favored of God* are those who admit their spiritual bankruptcy "in Adam" and their need of a Savior.[1] Such choice persons inherit everything in God's kingdom (all He has and all He is). They go from nothing to everything simply because they honestly and humbly confess their lack!

Throughout His brief ministry the Messiah opened many gateways to blessedness. But on Calvary the door swung open further than ever, because of the work that was accomplished there:

> Christ has redeemed us from the curse of the law by being made a curse for us—as it is written, "Cursed is everyone who hangs on a tree"—so that the blessing of Abraham might come on the Gentiles through Jesus Christ, that we might receive the promise of the Spirit through faith.
>
> —GALATIANS 3:13–14

After rising from the dead and ascending to heaven, on Pentecost, Jesus sent forth the Holy Spirit into the Upper Room and about one hundred twenty disciples were filled. It has since overflowed into every nation, language, and people group.

Now we who are born again need not beg, for God has already "blessed us with every spiritual blessing in the heavenly places in Christ" (Eph. 1:3). All of heaven's blessings—His love, His peace, His joy, His authority, His wisdom, His victory, and much more—have already been given to us. We possess these blessings by boldly confessing the promises and praising God for their manifestation.

However, in all of our getting, we need to maintain the mindset that still it is "more blessed to give than to receive" (Acts 20:35). In the parable of the sheep and the goats, from which we got our beginning verse, the status of being the "blessed of the Father" was not established by what believers *received*, but the far more excellent proof of what they *gave away to others*—such as visiting the sick or feeding the hungry (Matt. 25:31–46).

The ultimate state of blessedness will come to us when the Lord Jesus, our "blessed hope," returns in brilliant glory (Titus 2:13). Concerning that magnificent day, the promise has been given: "Blessed and holy is he who has part in the first resurrection. Over such the second death has no power" (Rev. 20:6, NKJV).

We will then be ushered into the millennial reign of the Messiah when the King will say to those sheep on His right hand: "Come, you *blessed of my Father*, inherit the kingdom prepared for you since the foundation of the world" (Matt. 25:34).

Once God completes His plan, thank God, "there shall be no more curse" (Rev. 22:3). Instead, there will only be "showers of blessings" (Ezek. 34:26).

DECLARE WHO YOU ARE IN CHRIST

I declare that I am one of the blessed of the Father! The Lord Jesus Christ has redeemed me from the curse. I am blessed spiritually, regenerated by the power of the Holy Spirit. I am blessed mentally, for God has given me a sound mind. I am blessed emotionally, for I am filled with the joy of the Lord. I am blessed materially, for God wishes above all things that I prosper. God has already blessed me with all spiritual blessings in heavenly places in Christ. But these things are not just for my benefit. I am blessed to be a blessing—to help others in the same way the almighty God has helped me. In Jesus's name, amen!

Additional reading: Genesis 2:3; Psalm 1:1–3; Matthew 5:1–11; Revelation 14:13; 19:9; 22:14

Chapter 9

THE BODY OF CHRIST

Now you are *the body of Christ* and members individually.
—1 Corinthians 12:27

A s all the varied parts of the human body work together in mutual interdependence, so should the body of Christ function. We may all have distinctly different roles, yet we are all essentially important. We need each other. We supply one another's needs, for the body is called to sustain itself.

> As we lovingly speak the truth, we will grow up completely in our relationship to Christ, who is the head. He makes the whole body fit together and unites it through the support of every joint. As each and every part does its job, he makes the body grow so that it builds itself up in love.
> —Ephesians 4:15–16, GW

The body of Christ should be linked by such a bond of covenant:

> That there may be no division in the body, but that the members may have the same care for one another. If one member suffers, all suffer together; if one member is honored, all rejoice together.
> —1 Corinthians 12:25–26, ESV

No envy. No jealousy. No rivalry. We are working together for a common cause and each member has its part to play. A hand cannot perform the function of a foot. An eye cannot perform the function of an ear. A tongue cannot perform the function of a nose. We are all unique, especially fitted for a specific task God has called us to fulfill. Yet far too often we seek to pattern our lives after others instead. In the process we just might lose ourselves. Abraham Lincoln recognized this dilemma and warned: "Every man is born an original, but sadly, most men die copies."[1]

God encourages us otherwise with exquisite words:

> The Lord looks from heaven; He sees all the sons of men.
> From the place of His dwelling He looks on all the inhabit-
> ants of the earth; He fashions their hearts individually.
>
> —PSALM 33:13–15, NKJV

When we get heavenly minded, we too will celebrate originality and individuality. When we do this, competition should come to a standstill and imitation should be greatly reduced. Instead our goal will be to perfect our distinctiveness in Christ as an act of worship to God and to be faithful to our particular role, as an act of selfless commitment to others.

Of course, we must have unity when it comes to foundational doctrines and the fulfilling of certain crucial biblical mandates. But unity becomes excessive and constrictive when it evolves too much into uniformity (notice the root word *uniform*—everyone appearing exactly alike). If the body of Christ is to be healthy, there must be a perfect blending of the two extremes. As the popular saying goes: "In essentials, unity; in non-essentials, liberty; in all things, charity."[2]

Within the human body completely different organs and parts fulfill completely different functions (e.g., the lungs, the heart, and the kidneys), yet all of these are supported by common elements (including the circulatory system, the muscular system, the nervous system, and the skeletal system) that unify the body and hold its individual, unique parts together. And so it is with us. Certain things hold us together, things upon which we are all equally reliant, including:

+ The blood of Jesus
+ The Word of God
+ The Spirit of God
+ Faith in God
+ Grace flowing from God

By these things we are unified.

> For as the body is one and has many parts, and all the many parts of that one body are one body, so also is Christ. For by one Spirit we are all baptized into one body, whether we are

Jews or Gentiles, whether we are slaves or free, and we have all been made to drink of one Spirit.

—1 Corinthians 12:12–13

What a mystery this is! In the kingdom of God "there is neither Jew nor Greek, there is neither slave nor free, and there is neither male nor female, for you are all one in Christ Jesus" (Gal. 3:28). We are made up of two genders, many ages, many races, many cultural groups, and many vocations in life, yet there are no gender barriers, no age barriers, no racial barriers, no cultural barriers, and no social barriers, for common sources flowing throughout the body result in a common faith, a common inheritance, and a common destiny. Beautiful!

Declare Who You Are in Christ

I declare that I am a member of the body of Christ! I am united with all other members by the blood of Jesus that cleanses us all, by the Word of God that feeds us all, by the Spirit of God that fills us all, and by the grace of God that saves us all. We are all unified by our common submission to the head, the Lord Jesus Christ. I celebrate this unity, yet simultaneously I also celebrate my own uniqueness. I will dare to fulfill the individual calling and purpose that God has fashioned for me to fulfill. I will also dare to celebrate the uniqueness of other fellow believers and be happy with what God has made each one of us to be. In Jesus's name, amen!

Additional reading: Romans 12:4–5; 1 Corinthians 10:16; 12:1–31; Ephesians 4:10–13

Chapter 10

THE CHILDREN OF ABRAHAM

They which are of faith, the same are the children of Abraham.
—GALATIANS 3:7, KJV

ABOUT FOUR THOUSAND years ago, when the Creator revealed Himself to a mid-eastern man named Abram, He initiated their relationship with a weighty demand and eight remarkable promises:

> Now the LORD said to Abram, "Go from your country, your family, and your father's house to the land that I will show you. I will make of you a great nation; I will bless you and make your name great, so that you will be a blessing. I will bless them who bless you and curse him who curses you, and in you all families of the earth will be blessed."
>
> —GENESIS 12:1–3

Most people identify themselves three ways: their national identity, their cultural identity, and their family identity. God commanded Abram to leave these things behind. In essence He was saying, "If you'll depart from familiar dependencies, I'll give you a completely new identity—and awaken purpose and destiny in you." Later on God even gave him a new name, Abraham, meaning father of a multitude, as a prophetic statement over his life. God still leads people like that.

How did this highly favored man respond to God? The Scripture explains, "By faith Abraham obeyed....He went out not knowing where he was going" (Heb. 11:8). So the divine design for his life was not revealed all at once. Abram had to walk it out one step at a time. God still works that way too.

When you respond to the true God as Abraham did, you become one of Abraham's spiritual children. He believed the word God spoke to him and followed God's instructions, and God made him a different person. In like manner when you believe and obey, you obtain a new identity and an inheritance, for "those who are of faith are blessed with faithful Abraham" (Gal. 3:9).

This legacy of blessing covers a lot of territory. The Lord "blessed Abraham in all things" (Gen. 24:1). He was "very wealthy in livestock, in silver and in gold," but more importantly he was also very rich in the things of God (Gen. 13:2). He was even called "the friend of God" (James 2:23).

At one point God told him to look up at the night sky and He made an awe-inspiring prediction: "Look up toward heaven and count the stars, if you are able to count them...so will your descendants be" (Gen. 15:5).

Such a glimpse into the future was "exceedingly abundantly beyond" anything Abraham and Sarah could have imagined—for they had not yet produced one child, much less a multitude (Eph. 3:20). But Abraham believed God, then something astonishing happened: God "credited it to him as righteousness" (Gen. 15:6).

This happened, not only for his sake, "but also for us," that righteousness might be "imputed to us who believe in Him who raised up Jesus our Lord from the dead" (Rom. 4:24, NKJV). Just as Abraham believed God *could* bring dead things back to life (Sarah's "dead" womb and his own "dead" body—see Romans 4:19–22), we believe and confess that God *did* bring something dead back to life (the Son of God who was crucified for us). As we express faith in God's power to resurrect, our dead souls are raised to life. Our sins are blotted out, and God grants to us also this amazing impartation—the "gift of righteousness" (Rom. 5:17).

THE ABRAHAMIC COVENANT

In this same visitation God solidified His commitment to Abraham with covenant language and symbolism. He instructed this great patriarch to take five different kinds of animals and offer them as sacrifices, dividing the larger ones in two parts:

> And it came to pass, when the sun went down and it was dark, that behold, there appeared a smoking oven and a burning torch that passed between those pieces. On the same day the

LORD made a covenant with Abram, saying: "To your descendants I have given this land, from the river of Egypt to the great river, the River Euphrates."

—GENESIS 15:17–18, NKJV

The almighty God condescended to implement a human ceremony commonly used in that era. When tribal companies made a league with each other, a sacrificial animal would be slain and the leaders would pass through the pieces of flesh. (See Jeremiah 34:18.) It was a gesture that their pact was as serious as death. Symbolically they were also calling death upon themselves if they broke covenant. The Bible never stated that Abraham passed between those pieces of flesh, but God did. It was an unforgettable way of declaring how utterly impossible it would be for His promises to fail, because God cannot die.

THE OVERFLOWING BLESSING

God revealed the ultimate impact of Abraham's life when He pledged that through him "all families of the earth will be blessed" (Gen. 12:3). This came to pass in a remarkable way. Toward the end of the old covenant God challenged the Israelites to be faithful in giving their tithe and offerings, saying:

Test Me now in this, says the LORD of Hosts, if I will not open for you the windows of heaven and pour out for you a blessing, that there will not be room enough to receive it

—MALACHI 3:10

Strangely, for four hundred years after this prophetic utterance, Israel never saw a time of overflowing blessing. In fact, it was quite the opposite. They were struggling just to survive, first dominated by the Grecian empire, and later by the Romans. Then one day, unexpectedly, in a remote desert area, it happened—a rough-looking prophet immersed a lowly Nazarene in the waters of Jordan:

And suddenly the *heavens were opened* to Him, and He saw the Spirit of God descending on Him like a dove.

—MATTHEW 3:16

The Abrahamic blessing that was poured out on the Messiah that day was too great to be contained within the banks of Judaism. The flood waters of grace increasingly rose higher for three-and-a-half years until they finally spilled over the edge into all the world, when the Messiah was crucified. Now we can boldly declare:

> Christ has redeemed us from the curse of the law by being made a curse for us...so that the blessing of Abraham might come on the Gentiles through Jesus Christ, that we might receive the promise of the Spirit through faith.
> —GALATIANS 3:13–14

It finally happened, just as God said it would. The Abrahamic blessing has surrounded the globe, and it daily abounds toward those who have accepted the seed of Abraham, Jesus Christ, the Son of God, as their Savior and Lord. (See Galatians 3:16.)

DECLARE WHO YOU ARE IN CHRIST

I declare that I am a child of Abraham! I am in covenant with the God of Abraham and the blessing of Abraham overflows my life. When I confessed that God raised Jesus Christ from the dead, I was resurrected spiritually, and like Abraham, I received the gift of righteousness. However, the primary evidence of the blessing of Abraham in my life is my ability to be a blessing and to help others understand the revelation of the God of Abraham. In Jesus's name, amen!

Additional reading: Genesis 17:1–27; 22:1–18; Romans 4:1–25; 2 Corinthians 5:21; Galatians 3:1–29; James 2:20–26

Chapter 11

INHERITORS OF HIS MOUNTAINS

I will bring forth descendants from Jacob, and out of
Judah *an inheritor of my mountains*; and My chosen
ones shall inherit it, and My servants shall dwell there.

—ISAIAH 65:9

WHEN TAKEN IN context, this verse is evidently a prediction of a new covenant people yet to come who would inherit God's mountains. First, God said He would "bring forth descendants from Jacob" (Isa. 65:9). *Jacob* is another name for Israel. According to Romans 11:17–24 all born-again believers are spiritually a part of Israel. We have been "grafted" into the olive tree of Israel if we have received Yeshua (Jesus) as our Messiah.[1]

Then God narrowed it down to the tribe of Judah. That's the tribe that Jesus belonged to—"it is evident that our Lord descended from Judah" (Heb. 7:14). In heaven He is even referred to as "the Lion of the tribe of Judah" (Rev. 5:5). Since we are Jesus's offspring, all who are saved—Jew or Gentile—can rightfully claim to be a spiritual continuation of this tribal family whose very name means *praise*.

There are two other identifying factors. This mountain-climbing, mountain-claiming status is given to God's "chosen ones" and those who fill the role of "servants" of God—those who selflessly serve His purposes (Isa. 65:9). These alone qualify to be inheritors of God's mountains. Those who are included will not just visit these peaks from time to time; they will dwell there all the days of their lives.

GOD'S HOLY MOUNTAINS

Not all mountains in this world qualify to be God's holy mountains, not even the most popular summits such as Everest, Kilimanjaro, or

Pikes Peak. These famous pinnacles may impress people with their majestic rise into the sky, but heaven has a different set of standards.

So what are the criteria? As we look back through the history of humanity, we discover certain "peak" moments when the Creator condescended to manifest Himself supernaturally on the earth. When He did, His covenant people were drawn upward into some towering height of divine revelation. Quite often these visitations took place on literal mountains, so that the natural paralleled the spiritual. All such scriptural summits are sacred sites: not to be worshipped, but to be deeply respected. They are holy mountains, both to God and to His people.

Grouped together, these holy mountains provide a foundation for our faith (a set of principles on which we can build our future) and a network of spiritual highways that successfully lead God-loving pilgrims from time to eternity. These two analogies are showcased in the following verses:

> His foundation is in the holy mountains.
> —Psalm 87:1, nkjv

> And I will make all My mountains a way, and My highways shall be exalted.
> —Isaiah 49:11, kjv

So let us visit these holy mountains in Scripture, declare them as a foundation for our lives and travel on these God-ordained highways toward the destiny that is unfolding before us all.

Seven Significant Summits

The following seven summits are probably the most significant in the Bible:

+ **Mount Ararat:** This is the holy mountain where the ark rested after the flood, where Noah and his family heard God's commitment to a covenant relationship with them, where the rainbow was seen, and where God smelled a sweet savor from Noah's burnt offering and lifted a curse from the entire world. (See Genesis 8:1–21.)

Those who inherit this mountain pass through the floods of tribulation in life. Not only do they survive; they also thrive by entering a covenant with the Creator. A rainbow of promise hovers over them, and the curse is lifted as God smells the sweet savor of worship in their lives.

+ **Mount Moriah**: This is the site where God tested Abraham in offering his son, Isaac, on an altar, a supreme act of self-sacrifice. God intervened, supplying a ram to take Isaac's place in death, a powerful picture of Calvary. Abraham named that place Yahweh-Yireh, meaning the Lord will see and provide. This was also the site where the temple of Solomon was built many years later.

   Those who inherit this mountain know the Father as their provider in every area of life; they know Jesus as their substitute in death; and they offer their bodies to the Holy Spirit as a temple in which He can dwell.

+ **Mount Sinai (or Horeb)**: This is the site where God declared the Ten Commandments with His thunderous voice and wrote them with His fiery finger on tablets of stone. Mount Sinai is also called Mount Horeb seventeen places in Scripture (probably because Horeb was either the mountain or the range, and Sinai, the highest peak, or something similar). Horeb is called "the mountain of God" in Exodus 3:1.

   Those who inherit Mount Sinai accept the moral and spiritual boundaries God sets for their lives; with His fiery finger He writes the law in their hearts.

+ **Mount Gerizim**: This is also known as the Mount of Blessing. Mount Gerizim was the location where six tribes of Israel, the offspring of free women (Leah and Rachel) to whom Jacob was married, shouted "amen" to the bless-ings of the law declared by the priests in the valley below, ending with the declaration, "The LORD will make you the head, and not the tail; you will only be above and you will not be beneath" (Deut. 28:13).

Those who inherit this mountain lay claim to all the blessings God promises in His Word, bringing them into a place of headship in their lives.

+ **Mount Olivet:** This is a limestone ridge about a mile long that covers the eastern side of Jerusalem, Mount Olivet is the site of several very significant biblical events: the triumphant entry of Jesus into Jerusalem, the blood-sweating prayer of Gethsemane, and the ascension of Jesus into heaven. At His return, Jesus will also descend on the Mount of Olives. (See Zechariah 14:4.)

  Those who inherit this mountain often share Jesus's Gethsemane prayer, "Not My will, but Yours be done!" (Luke 22:42); they also shout "Hosanna" in anticipation of His triumphant return.

+ **Mount Calvary:** This site is also called Golgotha, which means "the place of the skull," and is strangely in the actual shape of a human skull. It was there that Jesus became sin for us. Crowned with thorns, He bore on His brow the mental misery of a lost human race, and He tasted death for us all. Of all the holy mountains in and around Jerusalem, Calvary is the highest, in both a natural and spiritual sense.

  Those who inherit Calvary are "justified from everything from which you could not be justified by the Law of Moses" (Acts 13:39)—cleansed of all sin and set free from their past and the mind-crushing curse of their former lost state. The Messiah wore a crown of thorns there that we might receive a crown of life and a crown of righteousness. (See James 1:12; 2 Timothy 4:8.)

+ **Mount Zion:** David erected a tabernacle on Mount Zion to house the ark of the covenant when it was returned from the Philistines. On this mountain, twenty-four-hour-a-day worship took place, lavishing love on the Creator. There was no veil preventing the priests from viewing the ark and the Shekinah glory. It was a prophetic fore-shadowing of what will take place in the kingdom age to come, when Jesus will reign from Mount Zion. (See Psalm 48:1–2; Amos 9:11–13; Acts 15:15–18.)

Those who inherit Mount Zion live in the realm of worship and partake of the glory of God (See Hebrews 12:22–24.)

As we meditate on the meaning of each one of these holy mountains, may we climb up the slope, claim our inheritance, and shout words similar to Caleb of old: "God, give me this mountain in Jesus's name!"

DECLARE WHO YOU ARE IN CHRIST

I declare that I am an inheritor of God's mountains! Along with the rest of the body of Christ, I am an heir of the powerful revelation that took place on all of God's holy summits: Ararat, Moriah, Sinai, Gerizim, Olivet, Calvary, and Zion. I confess that all of these mountains are a mighty and immoveable spiritual foundation for my life and together they comprise a highway that will lead me from time into eternity. In Jesus's name, amen!

Additional reading: Exodus 15:17; Joshua 14:12; Psalm 125:1; Isaiah 11:6–9; 25:6–10; Daniel 2:31–45; Micah 4:1; Revelation 21:10

Chapter 12

THE JUST

The just shall live by his faith.
—HABAKKUK 2:4

ALL BELIEVERS SHOULD keep the glowing log of this verse burning in the hearth of their redeemed hearts. Why? Because these vitally important words were used by the Holy Spirit to birth a spiritual awakening that is still surrounding the globe with its influence. These words were originally received by the Prophet Habakkuk, a God-fearing Israelite who was desperately seeking answers from above. Grief-stricken over the wickedness and injustice so rampant in his day, the prophet cast himself in the role of a watchman, assuming personal responsibility for the spiritual condition of God's people. He declared before the Lord:

> I will stand at my watch and station myself on the watchtower; and I will keep watch to see what He will say to me.
> —HABAKKUK 2:1

God responded to him, saying:

> Write the vision and make it plain on tablets...for the vision is yet for an appointed time.... The just shall live by his faith.
> —HABAKKUK 2:2–4

Apparently these anointed words had little impact in Habakkuk's day, for they were reserved for "an appointed time." Like seed, they were planted in the soil of Judaism and remained dormant for centuries until the Messiah came. Once Jesus ascended to heaven, they finally germinated and sprang forth to help usher God's people into the age of grace.

Of all the apostles, Paul was the one God used most powerfully to show that "the law made nothing perfect, but the bringing in of a better hope did" (Heb. 7:19, KJV)—and that superior hope was the revelation that sinful human beings could be made righteous by faith in the Lord Jesus alone. In fact, Paul was the one who quoted Habakkuk when he wrote:

> For I am not ashamed of the gospel of Christ. For it is the power of God for salvation to everyone who believes, to the Jew first, and also to the Greek. For in it the righteousness of God is revealed from faith to faith. As it is written, "The just shall live by faith."
>
> —ROMANS 1:16–17

Another translation of this passage declares that the gospel is "God's plan for imparting righteousness to men, a process begun and continued by their faith" (PHILLIPS).

For sincere, God-loving Jews who were struggling to be righteous by human effort, by keeping the law and living a flawless life, this truth was revolutionary. That righteousness could be received, not just achieved, was an astounding thought. Of course, if it happened for Abraham, their patriarch, it could happen for them.

Strangely, after supernaturally helping to birth the new covenant age, after a while this revelation diminished in influence and was almost forgotten as the church slowly became steeped again in a righteousness-by-works mind-set and lifeless religious ceremonialism.

Hundreds of years later, though—in the sixteenth century—a Catholic monk named Martin Luther was struggling to find relief from the heaviness of his guilt-ridden heart. Regardless of what rituals or acts of self-denial he practiced, he still felt completely unacceptable in the sight of God. Then he read this passage where Paul quoted Habakkuk and was jolted into the realization that simple faith in the crucifixion and resurrection of the Lord Jesus would alone justify him (legally acquit him of all guilt—just as if he never sinned—and render him righteous in the sight of God). Describing that moment of divine revelation, Martin Luther penned,

> I felt myself to be reborn and to have gone through open doors into paradise.... This passage of Paul became to me a gate of heaven.[1]

The rest is history—church history—the history of real, heaven-sent revival, for that spark of divine inspiration in Martin Luther's heart ignited the combustible material of a European populace tired of religion and longing for a real relationship with God. Soon these words became a windswept fire of reformation blazing around the globe.

Now millions of converts to true Christianity fully understand the pathway to justification, the means by which lowly, sin-stained human beings can be included among "the just." Thankfully the following scriptures are often quoted now:

> Therefore, since we have been *justified by faith*, we have peace with God through our Lord Jesus Christ.
>
> —ROMANS 5:1

> But God demonstrates His own love toward us, in that while we were yet sinners, Christ died for us. How much more then, being now *justified by His blood*, shall we be saved from wrath through Him.
>
> —ROMANS 5:8–9

> Do you not know that the unrighteous shall not inherit the kingdom of God?…And such were some of you. But you are washed, but you are sanctified, but you are *justified in the name of the Lord Jesus and by the Spirit of our God.*
>
> —1 CORINTHIANS 6:9, 11, MKJV

> So that, being *justified by His grace* we might become heirs according to the hope of eternal life.
>
> —TITUS 3:7

So no matter how messed up your life has been, dare to believe these promises. God will restore you to a status of righteousness in the sight of heaven—just as if you never sinned. He will position you among "*the just*," granting you the righteousness which is "of God on the basis of faith" (Phil. 3:9). Then He will awaken within you a love for righteousness and empower you to live righteously as an act of worship to Him (which is the way it should be).

Yes, this amazing revelation is still a door to paradise and a gate to heaven. Look! It's swinging open for you right now. Walk through and—by faith—seize what is rightfully yours in Jesus's name.

DECLARE WHO YOU ARE IN CHRIST

I declare that I am one of the just who live by faith! I was dead in trespasses and sins, but the Son of God has resurrected me back to life spiritually. I confess that I believe in the power of His blood to wash away all sin. I believe in His grace. I believe in the name that is above every name—the Lord Jesus Christ. His Holy Spirit dwells within me. By these influences I am justified, reckoned righteous in the sight of heaven. As an act of grateful worship, I commit myself to walk in righteousness all of my days that I might be a praise to God in the earth. In Jesus's name, amen!

Additional reading: Job 25:4–6 (KJV); Acts 13:38–39; Romans 3:20–28; Galatians 2:16; 3:11–14; 5:1–4; James 2:20–24

Chapter 13

THE REDEEMED OF THE LORD

Let *the redeemed of the Lord* say so, whom He
has redeemed from the hand of the enemy.
—Psalm 107:2, nkjv

To redeem means to loose away or set free from bondage. It is a biblical term especially associated with the liberation of debtors, slaves, or prisoners. It can also mean to buy back that which has been lost, stolen, forfeited, or sold.

In the beginning Adam *lost* his oneness with God and passed on that fallen state to all his offspring. The enemy has since *stolen* many things from our hearts and lives: virtue, righteousness, peace, perfect health, and everlasting life. To one degree or another, we have all *forfeited* good things God wanted for us and in so doing *sold ourselves* into spiritual or mental enslavement—but thank God we learned to "say so": to declare our redemption rights and lay hold of them by faith.

From the onset God had a plan to redeem fallen humanity. Strangely, though, it took many centuries to unfold. The first mention of redemption is found in Genesis, the book of beginnings. As Jacob prayed over his grandsons, Ephraim and Manasseh, he declared:

> The Angel who has *redeemed me from all evil*, bless the lads; let my name be named upon them, and the name of my fathers Abraham and Isaac; and let them grow into a multitude in the midst of the earth.
>
> —Genesis 48:16, nkjv

The angel being referred to is no ordinary angel; it is "the Angel of the Lord," a title assigned to the pre-incarnate Messiah when He manifested Himself during the Old Testament era. (See Genesis 16:7; 22:11; Exodus 3:2; 23:23; Judges 6:11–24.)

Jacob was "saying so" as Psalm 107 suggests. He was declaring a spiritual law and precedent over his seed that when the Redeemer comes into the lives of His chosen ones, His intention is to deliver them from "all evil"—from every evil thing encountered in this world, even the bonds of death itself.

REDEEMED FROM THE LAW

When the law was revealed, it resulted in both blessings and curses on the children of Israel. For those who obeyed, it promised great blessings, but for those who disobeyed, terrible consequences. (Over one hundred curses are listed in Deuteronomy 27:14–26 and 28:15–68.) One disturbing verse announced unequivocally: "Cursed is he who does not confirm all the words of this law by doing them" (Deut. 27:26).

There were 613 commandments in the Torah (the first five books of the Bible), and according to this verse if a person fell short of keeping just one, he or she came under this curse of the law. So all who participated in the old covenant were under "a yoke of bondage," because no one could live a perfect life (Gal. 5:1). However, like the dawning of a new day, the new covenant arose out of the shadows with the promise:

> Christ has *redeemed* us from the curse of the law by being made a curse for us.
>
> —GALATIANS 3:13

What a miracle! Through His death and resurrection, Jesus paid a sufficient price in advance to loose all who would ever yield to His lordship from all the sins and failures, as well as the judgment that should have resulted. He has delivered us from every curse of the law, including sickness, poverty, and confusion of mind. He did not accomplish this miracle through some religious ritual.

> For you know that you were not *redeemed* from your vain way of life inherited from your fathers with perishable things, like silver or gold, but with the precious blood of Christ, as of a lamb without blemish and without spot.
>
> —1 PETER 1:18–19

Even if death stalks us, and it appears we may leave this world, we can echo the confident words of the patriarch Job, "I know that my Redeemer lives" (Job 19:25).

Whenever that may take place, God's redemptive plan will carry us through the portal of death to even greater glory at the second coming of the Lord and the resurrection of the dead. Therefore, "we also, who have the first fruits of the Spirit, groan within ourselves while eagerly waiting for adoption, the redemption of our bodies" (Rom. 8:23).

There is nothing to fear, for our God will never leave us nor forsake us until we arrive at this final goal. We have been "sealed with the Holy Spirit of promise" (Eph. 1:13, NKJV)—powerfully preserved by the Most High "for the day of redemption," the day when we are changed fully into His image (Eph. 4:30). The glory of Eden that was lost will then be regained.

No wonder our main scripture encourages God's redeemed to "say so" (Ps. 107:2). The key to experiencing all of these redemption rights is to seize them by faith through the power of the spoken word.

Let's do that right now!

DECLARE WHO YOU ARE IN CHRIST

I declare that I am one of the redeemed of the Lord! This is a past tense fact. By the blood of the Lamb, I have already been redeemed—loosed away from the bondage of sin, sickness, poverty, and all satanic plots against me. My mind has been redeemed. My emotions have been redeemed. My spirit, soul, and body have all been redeemed. I have even been redeemed from the power of the grave. If that is my lot, I will emerge from the dust victorious, glorified, and immortal. Until that magnificent day I declare that I will live in my redemption rights and overcome all things. In Jesus's name, amen!

Additional reading: Exodus 6:6; Isaiah 51:10–11; 54:5; 59:20; Jeremiah 31:11; Hosea 13:14; 1 Corinthians 1:30; Titus 2:14

Chapter 14

THE TEMPLE OF GOD

*Do you not know that you are the temple of God,
and that the Spirit of God dwells in you?*
—1 Corinthians 3:16

A T A CERTAIN point during the old covenant the hub of all spiritual activity in Israel was the temple of Solomon. Three times a year—during the feasts of Passover, Pentecost, and Tabernacles—the children of Israel traveled to the temple in Jerusalem to worship God and receive His blessing.

There was no building like the temple: overlaid with gold, decorated with jewels, adorned with images of cherubim, and housing the Shekinah glory of God. This celebrated structure, however, was not God's perfect purpose, nor His permanent plan. It was eventually destroyed.

Why would God allow such a glorious dwelling place to be demolished? Primarily because of sin and rebellion among the people of Israel, but also because He was not satisfied. A structure made of mortar, stone, and precious metals could not respond to Him with love. It could not express His divine nature or manifest His gifts. Only redeemed men and women under the new covenant could fulfill that need. So the temple was only a temporary step in the direction God really desired to go.

Being the temple of God is first a corporate inheritance, for the whole body of Christ makes up a singular temple. We, as "living stones, are being built up into a spiritual house as a holy priesthood to offer up spiritual sacrifices that are acceptable to God through Jesus Christ" (1 Pet. 2:5).

Being the temple of God is also a personal, individual inheritance, for each one of us is a separate "temple of the Holy Spirit," a unique "dwelling place of God" (1 Cor. 6:19; Eph. 2:22). So in essence, we are one corporate temple made up of many individual temples.

The Amazing Analogy

Almost three thousand years ago, gripped with worshipful wonder, Isaiah declared to the Most High: "Truly You are a God who hides Yourself, O God of Israel" (Isa. 45:15).

One way God hid Himself in the old covenant was to use certain things that happened in the natural to reveal supernatural realities destined to manifest under the new covenant. The temple of Solomon is a prime example. God knew from eternity past that His most-desired, eternal dwelling place would not be an inanimate building in the old covenant, but a blessed people who would invite him into their hearts in the new covenant. So in His genius He predetermined that His temporary habitation be filled with detailed symbols of what was yet to come. Here is a sampling of what He predetermined.

The temple site

Solomon's temple was erected on Mount Moriah, the very location where, many years prior, Abraham had offered his son, Isaac, as a sacrifice to God. In like manner the spiritual temple of God is built on the sacrifice of God's Son, for we could have never been indwelt by God were it not for the cleansing we have received through Jesus's blood.

The holy temple

This excellent edifice of worship was called the "holy temple" (Ps. 5:7). The word *holy* means sacred, separate from the world, and set apart for God. When we were born again, the new man or the "hidden person of the heart" was "created according to God in righteousness and true holiness" (1 Pet. 3:4, NKJV; Eph. 4:24). Of course, not only have we been made holy; we are also called to "be holy" (1 Pet. 1:16).

The three chambers

There were three sections to the temple: the outer court, the holy place, and the holy of holies. So also there are three parts to a redeemed person: the flesh, the soul, and the regenerated spirit. What took place in each of these sections corresponds to what God is doing in each part of us. So it follows that there are three kinds of Christians (fleshly, soulish, and spiritual) and three levels of fruit-bearing (thirtyfold, sixtyfold, or a hundredfold). (See Matthew 13:8.)

The furniture

There were eight different types of furnishings in the temple. In the outer court was the altar of sacrifice, the molten sea, and ten lavers; in the holy place were the ten tables of showbread, ten lamp-stands, and the altar of incense; and in the holy of holies were the ark of the covenant and the two cherubim facing outward on either side of the ark. Each piece of furniture bears its own prophetic message concerning our role as the temples of God:

+ **The altar of sacrifice:** This was the first piece of furniture encountered in the temple area, so our first step in approaching the Lord must be offering our "bodies as a living sacrifice, holy, and acceptable to God" (Rom. 12:1).

+ **The molten sea and the ten lavers:** These were containers of water used for cleansing; at the molten sea the priests washed, and at the lavers the sacrifices were washed. So God cleanses the church in our priestly and sacrificial service to Him "with the washing of water by the word" (Eph. 5:26).

+ **The ten tables of showbread:** The showbread was also called "the bread of the Presence," "the bread of face," and the "continual bread" because it was placed in the presence of God, before His face. (See Numbers 4:7, NKJV.)[1] It represents our calling to live before God, to seek His face, to abide in His presence continually, and to be living bread for Him (satisfying His hunger for fellowship) and living bread for the human race (satisfying their hunger for truth). (See Numbers 4:7; John 6:51; 1 Corinthians 10:17.) On each of the ten tables there were twelve loaves of unleavened showbread, representing the twelve tribes of Israel; also twelve times ten equals one hundred twenty—the number of disciples in the Upper Room. Being a fungus that spreads quickly, leaven represents sin, religious hypocrisy, and false doctrine. Therefore, to be spiritual showbread, we must live leaven-free lives. (See Matthew 16:11–12, NKJV; Mark 8:15, NKJV; Luke 12:1, NKJV; 1 Corinthians 5:6–8, NKJV.)

+ **The ten golden lampstands:** Each menorah was made up of five main parts: the golden vessel, the oil, the wicks, the fire, and the light. Each church in the book of the Revelation was represented as a golden menorah lampstand and so is every individual believer. (See Revelation 1:10–20, NKJV; Proverbs 20:27, NKJV.) Like the lampstand, each one of us should be a golden vessel filled with the oil of the Holy Spirit (the oil of joy—see Isaiah 61:3), with an upright will (the wick), and a heart on fire with passion for God. Thus we shed forth the light of truth. Each of the ten lampstands had seven bowls. Ten times seven equals seventy, the number of disciples Jesus originally sent forth to be the "light of the world" (Matt. 5:14).

+ **The altar of incense:** This represents our calling to seek the face of God. David said, "Let my prayer be set before You as incense" (Ps. 141:2). Incense emits its beautiful aroma only when it is set on fire. So our seeking of God must be on fire with holy passion as we offer up "spiritual sacrifices" of thanksgiving, joy, and praise to God (1 Pet. 2:5; see also Jonah 2:9; Psalm 27:6; Hebrews 13:15).

+ **The ark of the covenant:** When the ark was placed in the temple of Solomon (after the Philistines for a season had it in their control), it only contained the tablets of stone bearing the Ten Commandments written with the fiery finger of God. (See 2 Chronicles 5:10.) This represents how God writes His law in the hearts of believers that we might be His living epistles to the world. (See 2 Corinthians 3:1–3.)

+ **The mercy seat:** The lid of the ark was called "the mercy seat," yet no human being ever sat there. Since the glory of God rested on the ark, between the cherubim, we can assume it was God's seat—symbolically His throne on earth. (See Exodus 25:18.) Yet God's far greater desire is to actually enthrone Himself in us, to express His mercy through us and for the "riches of His glory" to rest upon us (Rom. 9:23; see also Psalm 22:3, NKJV).

The pillars of the temple

Finally there were two pillars flanking the door to the temple, one named Jakin (meaning "God will establish") and the other, Boaz (meaning "in Him is strength"). (See 1 Kings 7:21.)[2] In like manner, if we claim to be the temples of God, these two pillar-like confessions should stand tall on either side of the entranceway to our hearts: "God will establish us" and "in Him we are strong."

DECLARE WHO YOU ARE IN CHRIST

I declare that I am a temple of the Holy Spirit! God Himself dwells in me, and He expresses His nature and His gifts through me. I acknowledge that my regenerated spirit was created in true holiness. I am set apart for God's service. My life is on the altar. I am washed with His Word daily. I am bread for God and for the world. I accept the calling to be the light of the world. I am committed to passionate prayer rising as incense before His throne daily. My spirit is now the place where His mercy seat abides. God is now enthroned in me, His glory rests upon me, and He expresses His mercy through me to a world in great need. In Jesus's name, amen!

Additional reading: 2 Corinthians 6:14–16; Ephesians 2:19–22; Revelation 1:10–20; 8:1–6, (NKJV)[3]

PART 3

YOU ARE
TRANSFORMED

Chapter 15

CONVERTS

Zion shall be redeemed with judgment and
her *converts* with righteousness.
—Isaiah 1:27, kjv

Though the title *converts* is often used for God's people, it is found only once in the King James Version of the Bible. Triune in meaning the word describes someone who *turns away* from sin, *turns toward* God, and *returns* to a right relationship with Him. A number of spiritual influences work together to effect a true conversion, but the primary one is hearing God's Word. Psalm 19:7 asserts: "The law of the Lord is perfect, converting the soul."

The Hebrew word translated "law" in that passage is *Torah*, meaning the first five books of the Bible. If that portion of the Word of God was perfect under the old covenant to convert sinners into saints, how much more are all sixty-six books of the complete Bible, especially the last twenty-seven books of the New Testament.

Conversion is the key to true Christianity. It is a necessary part of a real salvation experience. While still on the earth Jesus told His chief disciples: "Truly I say to you, unless you are converted and become like little children, you will not enter the kingdom of heaven" (Matt. 18:3).

In other words He was warning that they must *turn away* from self-centered personal agendas, pride, and religious legalism; *turn toward* God with childlike humility and sincere love; and *return* to a right relationship with Him by grace. So it is for all of us.

Of course, once an initial conversion takes place, the process just begins. Every day contains many opportunities to:

+ *Turn away* from that which is ungodly and *turn toward* that which pleases God

+ *Turn away* from carnality and *turn toward* spirituality

+ *Turn away* from negative things (like doubt, depression, and hate) and *turn toward* their polar opposites (faith, hope, and love)

So let's allow the conversion process to take us beyond the initial experience of salvation into the full manifestation of what a son or daughter of God should be.

THREE PRIMARY REASONS

There are three primary reasons human beings should yield to the conversion process:

+ **It brings healing from past errors.** The early church leader James claimed that someone who "converts the sinner from the error of his way will save a soul from death and will cover a multitude of sins" (James 5:20).

+ **It opens up a door of blessing in the future.** After the crippled man at the beautiful gate was healed, Peter said to the crowd that gathered, "Repent and be converted, that your sins may be wiped away, that times of refreshing may come from the presence of the Lord" (Acts 3:19).

+ **It empowers us to help others.** Probably the greatest outcome of becoming a convert is the privilege and the responsibility of converting others. Each one of us should make the quality decision, "I was not converted to become overly introverted." We must refuse to be intimidated or shy; our job is too important.

Whenever God brings us out of a challenging time of life, we earn the right to reach back and deliver someone else from the same pit, but we must commit ourselves to the pursuit of this goal. A prime example from the Old Testament is Moses. Notice the three steps of conversion revealed in the three verses of Scripture:

By faith Moses, when he became of age, refused to be called the son of Pharaoh's daughter, choosing rather to suffer affliction with the people of God than to enjoy the pleasures of

sin for a time. He esteemed the reproach of Christ as greater riches than the treasures in Egypt, for he looked to the reward.
—HEBREWS 11:24–26

Moses *refused*, then he *chose*, then he *esteemed*. The next verse says, "He *forsook* Egypt" so there was a radical outcome, a dramatic conversion in his life (Heb. 11:27). He *turned away* from Egypt and its gods. He *turned toward* the truth; then he *returned* to a covenant relationship with the true God he inherited from his forefathers. The entire nation of Israel was impacted by this one man's conversion, and multiplied millions have been impacted since. Yes, a true conversion can bring exponential results.

David is also an excellent example, but from a different angle. In recovering from a backslidden state, David prayed for help, but he also promised that he would pass on that same grace of restoration to others. His words are quoted often:

> Create in me a clean heart, O God…Restore to me the joy of Your salvation…then I will teach transgressors Your ways, and sinners shall be converted to You.
> —PSALM 51:10, 12–13, NKJV

A powerful new covenant example is found in the conversation Jesus had with Peter right before He went to the cross:

> Simon, Simon, behold, Satan has desired you, that he may sift you as wheat. But I have prayed for you, that your faith fail not. And when you are converted, strengthen your brothers.
> —LUKE 22:31–32, MKJV

It happened just as Jesus prophesied. Peter failed (he denied the Lord), but his faith didn't fail (the Father answered Jesus's prayer!). Peter came out of the experience understanding God's forgiveness and more apt to pass forgiveness along to others. After it was all over, Peter was a stronger person and able to give strength away to others.

So no matter what you are going through right now, I prophesy to you, "It's all about conversion. It's an opportunity for you to change, and after you are converted, to strengthen others." So dare to glean all the positive change you can from the negative circumstances you're facing. Keep growing in faith and growing in God until that greatest of all conversions takes place on the day of the resurrection when all believers will be changed finally and totally into the glorious image of the Lord Jesus Christ.

DECLARE WHO YOU ARE IN CHRIST

I declare that I am one of Zion's converts! I have been brought out of darkness into God's marvelous light. I have turned away from the world, turned toward God, and returned to a relationship with Him. I make a commitment not to be selfish but selfless, not to be bitter but forgiving, not to be greedy but generous, not to be fearful but full of faith. I am no longer a child of darkness, but a child of the light; no longer a sinner, but a saint. I yield to this ongoing conversion process. Now my privilege and my responsibility is to reach out and convert others, helping them in some of the very same ways God has helped me. In Jesus's name, amen!

Additional reading: Jeremiah 31:18; Ezekiel 33:11; Joel 2:12; Acts 15:3

Chapter 16

A NEW CREATION

Therefore, if anyone is in Christ, he is *a new creation*; old things have passed away; behold, all things have become new.
—2 Corinthians 5:17, nkjv

Salvation in this new covenant era is not just based on religious behavioral modification; it is an act of re-creation. It is not achieved through human effort; it is received as a gift of God. It is not attained through "works of righteousness" (Titus 3:5); it is accepted by "faith" (Eph. 2:8). It is not the product of merely following religious rules; it is the result of a supernatural transformation.

This superb insight dominated Paul's teaching. Going against the grain of Messianic Jews who were still bound by the law, he dared to assert: "For in Christ Jesus neither circumcision nor uncircumcision means anything, but a new creation" (Gal. 6:15).

He understood that all of our religious rituals, traditions, and doctrines pale in comparison to the regenerative work of the Holy Spirit in our hearts. Even during the old covenant God enthusiastically looked forward to this new covenant era and testified:

> Also, I will give you a new heart, and a new spirit I will put within you. And I will take away the stony heart out of your flesh, and I will give you a heart of flesh. I will put My Spirit within you and cause you to walk in My statutes, and you will keep My judgments and do them.
> —Ezekiel 36:26–27

So in this age of grace, God doesn't just repair damaged hearts; He makes them brand new. Jesus referenced this mystery when He told Nicodemus, "You must be born again!" (John 3:7). The Greek word translated "again" in that passage is *anothen*, which literally means "from above."[1] In fact, *anothen* is actually translated "from above" in a number of scriptures, including John 3:31 and 19:11 and James 1:17. When we were born the first time, a new physical body came forth *from below*, from our mothers' wombs. When we are born again, apparently, a new spirit enters into us *from above* (from God). This regenerated, recreated spirit is in the likeness of God and imparts that image to us.

The very moment the blood of Jesus washes our hearts clean in spiritual rebirth, we are reconciled to God, made holy, and rendered righteous. How righteous, you might ask? The answer is astounding:

> God made Him who knew no sin to be sin for us, that we might become the righteousness of God in Him.
> —2 CORINTHIANS 5:21

We do not just *appear* as righteous as the firstborn Son in the eyes of the Father (imputed righteousness). We actually *receive* imparted righteousness. The result? No more guilt. No more shame. No more condemnation. And if we worshipfully, correctly, and gratefully respond, we no longer walk in carnality or worldliness. Two scriptures tell us what to do:

> That you put off, concerning your former conduct, the old man which grows corrupt according to the deceitful lusts, and be renewed in the spirit of your mind, and that you put on *the new man* which was created according to God, in true righteousness and holiness.
> —EPHESIANS 4:22–24, NKJV

> Do not lie to one another, since you have put off the old man with his deeds, and have put on *the new man* who is renewed in knowledge according to the image of Him who created him.
> —COLOSSIANS 3:9–10, NKJV

To be renewed is to be made brand new all over again. Whenever that happens, the new spirit within us gains ascendancy and the flesh part is brought under subjection. We also start thinking in a different and better way:

+ Instead of being focused on what we shouldn't do, we become focused on what we should do.

- Instead of being predominantly sin-conscious (aware of our failures), we are blessed to be righteousness-conscious (consciously aware that God has "made us worthy" [Col. 1:12, DRB]).

- Instead of fearfully cringing under the demands of the Ten Commandments of the old covenant (overshadowed by a curse), we joyously embrace the challenge of the two commandments of the new covenant: loving God with all our heart and loving our neighbor as ourselves (Matt. 22:36–40). If we truly love this way, we will automatically keep the other commandments for "love is the fulfillment of the law" (Rom. 13:10).

Thankfully this status of total victory is refreshed daily, even moment by moment. "For this reason we do not lose heart: Even though our outward man is perishing, yet our inward man is being *renewed* day by day" (2 Cor. 4:16).

Of course, the day will come when God will not only recreate us inwardly, but also outwardly—transforming "our body of humiliation, so that it may be conformed to His glorious body" (Phil. 3:21). Then this amazing God who renews His people will "renew" or recreate the entire universe, and there will be "new heavens and a new earth, in which righteousness dwells" (2 Pet. 3:13). No wonder, after such a climactic event, the saints will sing "a new song" (Rev. 14:3).

DECLARE WHO YOU ARE IN CHRIST

I declare that I am a new creation in Christ! Being "in Him," I partake of all that He is. I am infused with the character of the firstborn Son. Because of our union, I am "accepted in the Beloved," received in the presence of the Father (Eph. 1:6). I have been reconciled, restored to a right relationship with Him. I am filled with God's own righteousness. My Father has made me worthy to partake in the inheritance of the saints in light. With every passing moment the blood of Jesus flows through me, renewing the inward man—making me brand new all over again. For these reasons I declare that I have overcome the world. In Jesus's name, amen!

Additional reading: Psalms 51:10; 103:5; Ephesians 2:15

Chapter 17

THE POOR IN SPIRIT

Blessed are *the poor in spirit*, for theirs
is the kingdom of heaven.
—MATTHEW 5:3

THE NEW ENGLISH Bible translates this passage, "How blest are those who know their need of God." God's Word translation says, "Blessed are those who recognize they are spiritually helpless. The kingdom of heaven belongs to them."

Strangely in God's economy only those who admit their human deficiency can appropriate His divine abundance. Only those who acknowledge their bankrupt condition in Adam can go on to inherit the unsearchable riches of Christ. Only those who humbly confess, "Without Him I can do nothing," can then confidently declare, "I can do all things because of Christ who strengthens me" (Phil. 4:13; see also John 15:5). Those who comprehend this mystery can be bold in asserting, "When I am weak, then I am strong" (2 Cor. 12:10). What an empowering revelation this is!

God resists those who are proud and self-sufficient. The scripture did not say, "When the cocky and self-confident seek water, they will find it." Quite the contrary, Isaiah wrote, "When the poor and needy seek water, and there is none, and their tongues fail for thirst, I, the LORD, will hear them, I, the God of Israel, will not forsake them" (Isa. 41:17). Then God gives the astounding promise: "I will open rivers in high places, and fountains in the midst of the valleys; I will make the wilderness a pool of water, and the dry land springs of water" (Isa. 41:18).

What a miraculous transformation—from desertlike conditions to lush fruitfulness, from utter lack to lavish abundance, from an empty, dry soul to a heart overflowing with the river of God! And all it takes is humbly admitting our need with brokenness before God so that

He can mend our hearts and fill our lives with His grace. He has pledged to do His part; He is waiting for us to do ours.

INHERITING THE KINGDOM

Jesus pledged that the poor in spirit will inherit the kingdom of heaven (Matt. 5:3). But what does that encompass and when does that take place? Here are three important points:

+ The word *kingdom* simply means a king's domain: the realm, the people and the things over which a king rules. So the "kingdom of heaven" is comprised of all those things over which God rules, which are truly submitted to His authority.

+ The terms "kingdom of God" and "kingdom of heaven" are synonymous. One identifies God's domain by referring to the one who rules it (God), and the other does so by the place from which it is ruled (heaven).

+ We were "translated" into God's kingdom in a spiritual sense the very moment we were born again (Col. 1:13, KJV).

WHAT THE KINGDOM IS NOT

Two scriptures tell us what the kingdom is by telling us what it's not.

First, let's inspect Romans 14:17: "For the kingdom of God does not mean eating and drinking, but righteousness and peace and joy in the Holy Spirit."

So the kingdom is not about following dietary rules from the Torah; it's about experiencing the very heart of God. Often the personality of a kingdom resembles the personality of its king because it is shaped by his mind, heart, authority, and influence. So God's personality—His mind and heart—permeate His kingdom. Therefore, when we inherit the kingdom of heaven, we inherit all the personality traits of the great King whose presence permeates that kingdom. We acquire His wisdom, His grace, His knowledge, His power, and—as this passage states—His supernatural righteousness, peace, and joy. Such an acquisition is infinitely more important than Old Testament rules concerning eating and drinking.

Second, let's explore the meaning of 1 Corinthians 4:20: "For the kingdom of God is not in word, but in power."

In other words the kingdom of God is not just some whimsical, philosophical idea or curious, theological concept—it's a supernatural reality. When the kingdom manifests, there is a release of life-transforming power that can impart wholeness to the most broken soul and health to the sickest body. Although it can be explained in words, it far surpasses words. When experienced, it needs no explanation.

When Jesus sent forth His disciples two by two to the cities He intended to visit, He commanded them to preach "the kingdom of heaven is at hand," but then He added, "Heal the sick, cleanse the lepers, raise the dead, and cast out demons. Freely you have received, freely give" (Matt. 10:7–8).

In other words Jesus was conveying, "Tell them about the kingdom, how God can reign in their lives in supernatural power, but then, do something far better—demonstrate His dominion by manifesting miracles, signs, and wonders!" If it worked then, it will still work in this hour.

DECLARE WHO YOU ARE IN CHRIST

I declare that I am called to be one of the poor in spirit! Therefore, I admit that I am bankrupt, empty, and incomplete without the Lord Jesus, but in Him I am rich, I am full, and I am complete. He is the vine and I am one of His branches. Without Him I can do nothing, but through Him I can do all things, for He transfers His love and strength and power to me. The essence of the kingdom of heaven is flowing through me now, the very attributes of the King of that kingdom manifesting in my heart and life. I pray for this by saying, "Father, Your kingdom come, Your will be done, on earth as it is in heaven." In Jesus's name, amen!

Additional reading: Psalm 40:17; Matthew 5:10; 16:19; 2 Corinthians 8:9; James 2:5

Chapter 18

THE RICH OF THE EARTH

All *the rich of the earth* will feast and worship; all
who go down to the dust will kneel before him.
—Psalm 22:29, niv

PSALM 22 CONTAINS some of the most detailed predictions
of the crucifixion of Jesus to be found in the Old Testament.
Consider just the following three:

+ It includes one of the seven statements Jesus made on the
cross—"My God, My God, why have You forsaken Me?"
(Ps. 22:1, fulfilled in Matthew 27:46).

+ It foretells how the soldiers would gamble over His
clothing—"They part My garments among them, and cast
lots for My clothes" (Ps. 22:18, fulfilled in Mark 15:24).

+ It explains in advance how He would be torturously
killed—"They pierced My hands and My feet" (Ps. 22:16,
nkjv, fulfilled in John 19:37; 20:25–26).

After such graphic descriptions of the Messiah's execution, the
psalmist then foretells the way that believers will benefit:

The poor will eat and be satisfied; those who seek the Lord will
praise him—may your hearts live forever! All the ends of the
earth will remember and turn to the Lord, and all the families of the nations will bow down before him, for dominion
belongs to the Lord and he rules over the nations. *All the rich
of the earth will feast and worship*; all who go down to the dust
will kneel before him.
—Psalm 22:26–29, niv

Notice that both the first and last sentence of the passage above
speak of "eating" something as a result of Jesus's death on Calvary.

What kind of meal did God provide through the suffering of His Son? Jesus Himself explained:

> I am the living bread which came down from heaven. If anyone eats of this bread, he will live forever. The bread which I shall give for the life of the world is My flesh.
>
> —JOHN 6:51

During the Last Supper, He continued unveiling this mystery:

> As they were eating, Jesus took bread, blessed it and broke it, and gave it to the disciples and said, "Take and eat. This is My body." Then He took the cup, and after He gave thanks, He gave it to them, saying, "Drink of it, all of you. For this is My blood of the new covenant, which is shed for many for the remission of sins."
>
> —MATTHEW 26:26–28

Jesus's sacrificial death, burial, resurrection, and ascension to heaven made it possible for those who believe to "eat" of His flesh and "drink" of His blood in a spiritual sense, thus becoming one with Him forever. This happens in a much more profound way than just partaking of the communion ritual. That ceremony is only a symbol of something far more important.

Jesus was the Word made flesh (John 1:14). Therefore, to eat His flesh means to eat His Word, digesting truth into our innermost being. When we eat food, it becomes a part of us. Spiritually speaking, when we eat the Word, it also becomes a part of us—so much so that we each become an expression of His Word in this world—a living epistle, the "letter of Christ"—"known and read by all men" (2 Cor. 3:2–3).

The communion ritual also involves ingesting Jesus's blood. The Old Testament reveals "the life of the flesh is in the blood" (Lev. 17:11). Therefore, the life of God is in the blood of God, and if God ever had blood, it was in the veins of His Son. (See Acts 20:28.) Therefore, to drink His blood is to drink in His life-giving Spirit: His nature, His attributes, His very essence.

By partaking of this spiritual meal (the Word and the Spirit) we are truly feasting with God as we journey through this wilderness world. As we eat this incomparably sumptuous, spiritual banquet, we partake of all the blessings and benefits of the new covenant. In so doing, we are eternally prospered through God's promises and provisions. In other words we receive "true riches" (Luke 16:11).

> For the same Lord over all is rich to all who call upon Him.
> —ROMANS 10:12, NKJV

Paul put a spiritual magnifying glass on how this powerful transition took place for us:

> For you know the grace of our Lord Jesus Christ, that though He was rich, yet for your sakes He became poor, that through His poverty you might be rich.
> —2 CORINTHIANS 8:9

What does that mean—Jesus "became poor"?

Well, what made the Son of God rich? Stocks, bonds, real estate, corporate holdings, a large bank account? Of course not! The Son of God was rich in the splendor of heaven, rich in intimate fellowship with the Father, rich in the adoration of angels, rich in the undisturbed peace of heaven, and much, much more. But He divested Himself of all those supernatural riches to assume the poverty-stricken form of human flesh to rescue us.

When He went to the cross, He was reduced to even greater poverty as a result of becoming "an offering for sin" (Isa. 53:10). The one thing that enriched Him while He was on the earth (the presence of the Holy Spirit) departed from Him as He tasted "death for every man" (Heb. 2:9, KJV). Yet through His poverty those who believe are made rich in a number of ways:

+ Rich in God's goodness: "Do you despise the riches of His goodness, tolerance, and patience, not knowing that the goodness of God leads you to repentance?" (Rom. 2:4).

+ Rich in faith: "Listen, my beloved brothers. Has God not chosen the poor of this world to be rich in faith?" (James 2:5).

+ Rich in God's glory: "In order to make known the riches of His glory on the vessels of mercy, which He previously prepared for glory" (Rom. 9:23).

- Rich in grace: "In Him we have redemption through His blood and the forgiveness of sins, according to the riches of His grace" (Eph. 1:7).

- Rich in the Word: "Let the word of Christ dwell in you richly in all wisdom" (Col. 3:16).

By receiving this abundance of spiritual wealth, we will ultimately serve as eternal proof of the indescribable generosity of our heavenly Father:

> That in the ages to come He might show the exceeding riches of His grace in His kindness toward us in Christ Jesus.
>
> —EPHESIANS 2:7, NKJV

DECLARE WHO YOU ARE IN CHRIST

I declare that I am one of the rich of the earth! I was born into this world spiritually poverty stricken, but through the cross I have been lifted into spectacular wealth beyond description. God has enriched my life with the gift of repentance, the gift of faith, the gift of grace, the gift of His glory, the gift of the Word of God, and the gift of eternal life. By these heavenly deposits I have been raised from spiritual bankruptcy and degradation into the "incomprehensible riches of Christ" (Eph. 3:8). Now my worshipful response is be "rich toward God" and "rich in good works" toward others (Luke 12:21; 1 Tim. 6:18). In Jesus's name, amen!

Additional reading: Proverbs 10:22; Jeremiah 15:16; Ephesians 2:4; 1 Timothy 6:17–19; Revelation 5:12

Chapter 19

SAINTS

> To the church of God which is at Corinth, to those
> who are sanctified in Christ Jesus, called to be
> *saints*, with all who in every place call on the name
> of Jesus Christ our Lord, both their Lord and ours.
> —1 Corinthians 1:2

THE WORD SAINT has traditionally been used to refer only to those Christians who reach a high degree of devotion to God—those who live exceptionally disciplined, holy, and pious lives. However, our primary verse of Scripture above throws the gate wide open, giving three simple criteria for inclusion in this elite group:

+ **Saints are members of "the church of God":** The word "church" is from the Greek word *ekklésia* (pronounced ek-klay-see'-ah) meaning called out ones.[1] Therefore, "the church of God" is comprised of all those who have been called "out of darkness into His marvelous light," called out of a life of sin and selfishness into a life of holiness and unselfish love (1 Pet. 2:9).

+ **Saints are those who are "sanctified in Christ Jesus":** The word *sanctified* has a triune meaning: to be cleansed from the defilement of sin, made holy, and dedicated to God for His sacred purposes.[2]

+ **Saints "call on the name of Jesus Christ":** This is as simple as it gets. All who call on the name of the Lord to be saved are subsequently called by God to be saints. Period. No exclusions. Across the board. Everyone in the church.

All who have been born again, regardless of denominational affiliation, are included. Wow! In an age when much of the church is overtaken by compromise, apathy, and spiritual lukewarmness, isn't this a somewhat audacious thing to consider? Could it be a personal wake-up call to you and me?

SAINTHOOD AND SANCTIFICATION ARE ONE

Sainthood and sanctification are inseparably interwoven because on a foundational level, a saint is someone who has been sanctified. This spiritual status initially comes as a gift from God. When we confess Jesus as Lord of our lives, a number of elements work together simultaneously to sanctify us, or to present us holy unto the Lord. At that pivotal moment we are:

+ "Sanctified by the truth" (John 17:19)
+ "Sanctified by faith" in Jesus (Acts 26:18)
+ "Sanctified by the word of God and prayer" (1 Tim. 4:5)
+ "Sanctified...in the name of the Lord Jesus" (1 Cor. 6:11)
+ "Sanctified through the offering of the body of Jesus Christ once for all" (Heb. 10:10).
+ "Sanctified" by the blood of Jesus (Heb. 13:12)
+ "Sanctified by the Holy Spirit" (Rom. 15:16)
+ "Sanctified...by God the Father" (Jude 1:1)

So this is how it works (going down this list in the order just presented). First, we hear the truth, then faith is awakened in our hearts. We respond by confessing God's Word and praying the prayer of salvation. We call on the name of Jesus and receive the benefits of His broken, crucified body. All our sins are forgiven. The blood of Jesus cleanses us and the Holy Spirit sets us apart, sealing us and dedicating us to God. The Father then positions us as sons and daughters in His family, and we are consecrated to His divine purposes. As a repentant person passes through these steps one by one, *voila! Instantly! Out comes a saint!*

Well, yes and no. To say it that way is like lifting up an acorn and claiming it is actually an oak tree. It is, but it isn't. It may have the identity, the hidden image, and the amazing potential, but to really be an oak tree, that acorn has to fall "into the ground and die" and then spend a good deal of time growing (John 12:24).

And so it is with us. All believers have the identity and the inheritance of being saints, but to really be saints in a manifest way—to see this inner potential fully awakened—we must die to self, die to the world, and die to sin. Then we must spend a good deal of time growing in God.

Any denial of self will be well worth it, for the end result is glorious. Paul revealed that ultimately "the saints will judge the world" and "judge angels" (1 Cor. 6:2–3). The Old Testament prophet Daniel caught a prophetic glimpse of our final destiny, after the Antichrist is defeated and this present age comes to a close:

> Then the kingdom and dominion, and the greatness of all the kingdoms under the whole heaven, shall be given to the people of *the saints of the Most High*, whose kingdom is an everlasting kingdom, and all dominions shall serve and obey Him.
>
> —DANIEL 7:27

In that day we will meet the "King of saints" face-to-face and thank Him profusely for paying the necessary price that we might be changed into His saintly image (Rev. 15:3).

DECLARE WHO YOU ARE IN CHRIST

I declare that I am a saint of the Most High God! I have been sanctified by God, cleansed from sin, made holy and set apart for His sacred purposes. I refuse to be contaminated by the world. I repent of all sin and claim the blood of Jesus cleansing me and making me pure in the sight of God. I surrender completely to the King of saints and to the purpose that He has placed in my life. I look forward to the grand and glorious day when the saints will possess the kingdom and the whole world will be holy unto the Lord. In Jesus's name, amen!

Additional reading: Psalms 31:23; 50:5 (KJV); 116:15 (KJV); Ephesians 5:25–27; Colossians 1:12

Chapter 20

THE STRONG

Therefore, I will divide Him a portion with the great,
and he shall divide the spoil with *the strong*, because
he poured out his soul to death, and he was numbered
with the transgressors, thus he bore the sin of many
and made intercession for the transgressors.

—Isaiah 53:12

I SAIAH 53 IS another of the premier passages in the Old Testament foretelling the crucifixion of the Son of God and the wondrous things that would result. Similar to Psalm 22, it contains some of the most quoted prophecies concerning the Messiah's mission and conquest. Ironically it is stated in the past tense, though it was yet future at the time it was written (surely God's way of showing that it would inevitably come to pass). Consider the following three verses:

> Surely He has borne our grief and carried our sorrows; yet we esteemed Him stricken, smitten of God, and afflicted. But He was wounded for our transgressions, He was bruised for our iniquities; the chastisement of our peace was upon Him, and by His stripes we are healed. All of us like sheep have gone astray; each of us has turned to his own way, but the LORD has laid on Him the iniquity of us all.
>
> —Isaiah 53:4–6

Then in the final verse of the chapter the Father foretells the glorious outcome:

> Therefore, I will divide Him a portion with the great, and He shall divide the spoil with *the strong*, because He poured out His soul to death.
>
> —Isaiah 53:12

Mysteriously God refers to those who will benefit from the cross as "the strong," though prior to that pivotal event, all who are unsaved could rightly be termed "the weak." Why is that? Because we were born into this world under the curse of Adam, under the curse of the law, under the dominion of sin, under the control of satanic powers, under the influence of a fallen nature, and under the inescapable shadow of death. Helpless and hopeless, vulnerable and defenseless, defeat was inevitable for all of us. But then the "strong Lord" came down to our frail level, identifying with us in our low estate that we might be lifted up to His exalted state: seated with Christ in heavenly places (Ps. 89:8, KJV; see also Ephesians 2:6).

WHAT DOES *SPOIL* MEAN?

In our featured verse, the Father declares that He will "divide the spoil with *the strong*," but what is meant by "the spoil"?

The normal definition is plunder or booty taken from an enemy defeated in battle. Colossians 2:15 announces that at the cross Jesus "spoiled principalities and powers" (KJV) and "made a public spectacle of them, triumphing over them in it" (NKJV). In other words, through His death the Son of God stripped "principalities and powers" of their most valued possessions. Most likely this is a reference to high-ranking evil spirits, assigned to regions, nations, and cities, who shared legal authority over various spheres of influence in the earth. In the fall of mankind Adam relinquished the authority over this world to Satan, the evil angel Jesus later referred to as "the ruler of this world" (John 12:31). But our Redeemer has restored dominion to those who receive forgiveness through His blood. Thus He vanquished (spoiled) the enemy by taking back what Adam lost.

Now we have dominion over sin, over satanic powers, over the flesh, over the curse of Adam, over the curse of the law, over death, over the grave, and over hell—over all the enemies of the human race. Through our identification with the crucified One, we are cleansed. Through our identification with the risen One, we are raised to a position of spiritual supremacy and victory.

No wonder God refers to new covenant sons and daughters of God as "the strong"—for He has made us stronger than all our adversaries. Hebrews 11:34 explains that "out of weakness" God's people are "made strong." This impartation has happened many ways, but the following three are emphasized especially in Scripture.

Strong in faith

Abraham had a promise from God that he would sire a son in his old age. Admirably Abraham "staggered not at the promise of God through unbelief; but was *strong in faith*, giving glory to God" (Rom. 4:20, KJV). "He considered not his own body now dead...neither yet the deadness of Sara's womb," but believed that the prophetic word he received from God would come to pass (Rom. 4:19, KJV). We too must not even consider those things that are pitted against the purpose of God in our lives, but be strong in affirming both the written Word (the Bible) and the living Word (communications we have personally received from God).

Strong in grace

Paul encouraged his pastor protégé, Timothy, saying, "My son, be *strong in the grace* that is in Christ Jesus" (2 Tim. 2:1). Grace is unmerited love and divinely imparted ability. In other words the apostle was revealing that God's love over Timothy's life and the spiritual gifts that had been awakened in him were his source of strength, not his human abilities or willpower. And so it is with us.

Strong in the Lord

Ephesians 6:10 encourages us to "*be strong in the Lord* and in the power of His might." If we have made Jesus Lord of our lives, He is the head, and we are members of His body. In that mystical union all that the firstborn Son is and all that He has passes to us. For instance, Romans 8:2 states, "The law of the Spirit of life in Christ Jesus has set me free from the law of sin and death." Therefore, just as the resurrection life of God lifted Jesus out of the grips of death, if we abide in Him, the resurrection life of God will abide in us and death-dealing errors from our past cannot hold us in their grip. So our source of strength is our position "in Christ Jesus." (Other examples: 2 Corinthians 1:20; 2:14; Ephesians 2:13; Philippians 3:9; and Colossians 1:28.) If we are sincere toward God, we can instead courageously confess, as Micah 7:8 says, "Rejoice not against me, O mine enemy: when I fall, I shall arise; when I sit in darkness, the LORD shall be a light unto me" (KJV; see also Romans 8:11; 1 John 2:27).

Of course, these sources of strength may remain relatively untapped unless we implement Joel's exhortation:

> Let the weak say, "*I am strong.*"
>
> —JOEL 3:10, NKJV

So lift your voice. Be bold. The power of death and life are in your tongue. Even when you feel weak, rise up in the Spirit and dare to say:

> I can do all things through Christ who strengthens me
>
> —PHILIPPIANS 4:13, NKJV

DECLARE WHO YOU ARE IN CHRIST

I declare that I am one of the strong! I am who God says I am. Greater is He who is within me than he who is in the world. My enemies have all been spoiled, stripped of their power. Satan no longer has authority over me, sin no longer has dominion over me, and death no longer controls me. I refuse to consider any negative thing. Instead I will be strong in faith, strong in grace, and strong in the Lord and the power of His might. Yes, I dare to say, "If God is for me, who and what can be against me." In Jesus's name, amen!

Additional reading: Psalm 27:14; Isaiah 35:4; 40:29–31; Jeremiah 31:11; Matthew 11:12; 1 Peter 5:10

Chapter 21

VESSELS OF MERCY

> What if God, willing to show His wrath and to make
> His power known, endured with much patience the
> vessels of wrath prepared for destruction, in order to
> make known the riches of His glory on the *vessels of
> mercy*, which He previously prepared for glory?
> —ROMANS 9:22–23

A VESSEL IS an object intentionally created to be filled with some kind of substance. There are many kinds of vessels in our homes: pots, pans, bowls, glasses, cups, and so on—each with its own specific function. In like manner, human beings are vessels created with the unique spiritual capacity of being "filled."

Some choose to be filled with dark, sinful tendencies—attitudes such as rebellion, lust, anger, and selfishness. Others appeal to the God of heaven to be filled with His nature—love, joy, peace, wisdom, grace, and power. Of course, we desire not just to be filled with godlike traits, but also with God Himself, with His personal presence. Only then can we fulfill the divinely authored design for our lives. But what happens when there have been deep failures preventing the fulfillment of the divine purpose in the past? That's when mercy arrives as a beacon in the night.

WHAT IS MERCY?

Mercy is compassion shown especially to offenders or those of criminal behavior. It is pity extended toward the guilty, even though judgment is deserved. Normally the dispensing of mercy hinges on sincere remorse and desire for change.

Mercy is a dominant character trait in the personality of God, who described Himself to Moses as "the LORD, the LORD God, merciful and gracious…keeping mercy for thousands" (Exod. 34:6–7).

During that era God also gave the design for something called the tabernacle, a humble, tentlike structure where the divine presence resided and where God's people came to worship and seek His favor. The tabernacle had three chambers: the outer court, the holy place, and the holy of holies. In the innermost chamber was the ark of the covenant.

The two tablets of stone on which God wrote the Ten Commandments were in the ark. (The book of the law was also either in the ark or at its side.) (See Deuteronomy 10:1–5; 31:26.) This revelation (the Torah) was later called "the ministry of condemnation" and "the ministry of death," because of the serious judgments pronounced on those who failed to live up to its standard (2 Cor. 3:7, 9, NKJV). However, there was one thing in the holy of holies that was positioned higher than the law, and that was the lid of the ark—mysteriously called "the mercy seat" (Exod. 25:17). No man ever sat there, but on the lid, between the cherubim, God's glory rested. In a sense it was God's representative throne on earth—a revelation of His heart—that on the highest level He was not just a stern judge, but "the Father of mercies," and erring human beings could appeal to Him (2 Cor. 1:3).

THE MAIN REQUIREMENT

One primary attitude that attracts the mercy of God is the fear of the Lord. This is not a crippling kind of fleshly fear, but a deep reverential awe toward the Creator. It is the highest expression of respect for God's highness, God's holiness, God's greatness, and God's majesty. Those who cultivate this quality of character are given wonderful promises.

> For as the heavens are high above the earth, so great is His mercy toward those who fear Him.
>
> —PSALM 103:11

Consider just how high "the heavens" must be. Scripture teaches there are three heavens. (See 2 Corinthians 12:2–4.) The first heaven is probably comprised of the atmosphere around the earth and the physical universe beyond. The second heaven is a higher spiritual realm filled with angelic and demonic activity. The third heaven, called paradise, is the dwelling place of God, where the fullness of His glory manifests. Possibly the third heaven is just as infinite and endless as the God who dwells there. If that be so, then above the one who fears the Lord is an infinitely inexhaustible reservoir of mercy.

Six verses later in Psalm 103 we find another great promise: "But the mercy of the LORD is from everlasting to everlasting upon those who fear Him" (Ps. 103:17).

Now we have a slightly different perspective—from the infinite past to the infinite future there is no break in the amount of mercy available for that person who reverences God to the highest degree. It weaves its way through all the negatives of yesterday, even the moment we were conceived in sin, and through all the challenges of tomorrow, even death itself. (See Psalm 51:5.) Mercy will prevail over it all.

There is a beautiful word picture implied in these two verses from Psalm 103. The first image is vertical, with mercy stretching from earth to the highest heaven. The second image is horizontal, with mercy stretching from eternity past to eternity future. So in a figurative sense, those two comparisons form a cross, which itself is the greatest symbol of mercy ever to hover over a wayward and needy human race.

Praying for Mercy

There are many key miracles and deliverances in the Gospels that happened when desperate people prayed for the Lord's mercy:

+ The woman of Canaan whose daughter was possessed with a demon prayed, "Have mercy on me, O Lord, Son of David" and her child was delivered (Matt. 15:22).

+ Blind Bartimaeus cried out, "Jesus, Son of David, have mercy on me" and he received his sight (Mark 10:47).

+ The ten lepers pled, "Jesus, Master, have mercy on us" and they were cleansed (Luke 17:12, NKJV).

None of these individuals went through a faith seminar in which they learned to confess the promises of God and to bind and loose, taking authority over their circumstances (which are all good things to do). They merely cried out for mercy, and the heart of God was touched to such degree that real miracles happened. Jesus still stands in the gap for those who are in need. He is "a merciful and faithful High Priest in the things pertaining to God" (Heb. 2:17). If He healed and delivered when He walked the earth, He will surely do it again. He is "the same yesterday, and today, and forever" (Heb. 13:8).

> Let us therefore come boldly to the throne of grace, *that we may obtain mercy* and find grace to help in time of need.
> —HEBREWS 4:16, NKJV

DECLARE WHO YOU ARE IN CHRIST

I declare that I am a vessel of mercy! God has canceled my guiltiness and poured out His compassion on my life. Because I fear the Lord, I have nothing left to fear—for as high as the heavens are above the earth, so great is His mercy toward me. He is "the God of my mercy" (Ps. 59:10, KJV). He feels my pain as if it was His own, and He assures me that a new beginning is always possible. I will arise victorious out of the failures and hurts of my past, for "mercy triumphs over judgment" (James 2:13). In great gratitude, I offer my heart to God as His throne so that through me He can generously extend mercy to others. In Jesus's name, amen!

Additional reading: Deuteronomy 7:9; 2 Chronicles 5:13–14; 6:42; 7:1–3; Psalm 136:1–26 (KJV); Luke 1:68–72; Titus 3:5

PART 4

YOU ARE CALLED

Chapter 22

THE CALLED OF JESUS CHRIST

Among whom you also are *the called of Jesus Christ.*
—ROMANS 1:6, NKJV

EVERY CHILD OF God has a calling—a God-authored purpose in life. The scripture above was addressed not just to the leadership of the church in Rome, but also to every individual member. Actually it reaches much further, for the Holy Spirit inspired Paul to write those words, knowing that one day it would be a message and a revelation for millions of born-again believers all around the globe.

SO WHAT ARE WE CALLED TO DO?

If you were a Christian around the turn of the millennium, chances are at one time or another, you may have worn a bracelet or a T-shirt bearing the letters WWJD, an acronym for the challenging question, "What Would Jesus Do?" The answer is the very same things that He did—He ministered to the whole spectrum of society, to the downtrodden and the well-to-do, the ostracized and the popular, the illiterate and the educated, the sinful and the holy, and the weak and the strong. He ministered to good people such as Nicodemus, but He also hung out with bad people, loving them *where they were* in order to get them *where they needed to be.* He reached out to every class of people, preaching the gospel to the meek, speaking the truth, forgiving the erring, delivering the oppressed, healing the sick, feeding the hungry, and even raising the dead.

The Son of God is not here now (physically speaking), but we are—and He lives in us. *So what are we called to do?* The same kinds of things that He would do if He were here in a physical form Himself. Just as He showed love to the unlovely, the unloving, and the unlovable, so we are called to be expression of His love in this world. Yes, we need to be His heart expressed, His hands extended, and His voice sounding out in this present era.

THE THREE LEVELS

There are three primary levels to the calling of God:

1. The whole world is called to salvation: "Turn to Me and be saved, all the ends of the earth. For I am God, and there is no other" (Isa. 45:22).

2. The church as a whole is called for the general purpose of being transformed into the Lord's likeness: "And we know that all things work together for good to those who love God, to those who are *the called according to His purpose*. For whom He foreknew, He also predestined to be conformed to the image of His Son, that He might be the firstborn among many brethren" (Rom. 8:28–29, NKJV; see also 2 Corinthians 3:18).

3. Each individual Christian is called to fulfill a distinct purpose in advancing and establishing the kingdom of God in this world: "The Lord looks from heaven.... From the place of His dwelling He looks on all the inhabitants of the earth; He fashions their hearts individually" (Ps. 33:13–15, NKJV).

Each person is totally unique, handmade by the Creator, and once that person is saved, his or her uniqueness is enhanced supernaturally. God's power overlaps natural abilities to make that person *the best there is* at fulfilling a particular part of the plan of God.

> Who has saved us and *called us with a holy calling*, not according to our works, but according to His own purpose and grace which was given to us in Christ Jesus before time began.
> —2 TIMOTHY 1:9, NKJV

So before the earth was even spinning on its axis, the Creator gave you a specific "purpose." In advance He also gave you enough "grace" (divinely imparted ability) to fulfill that "purpose." So you will never face any situation in life in which you lack the sufficient divine empowerment not only to survive but also to thrive. Knowing this should build unshakable confidence in you that you truly can know and fulfill the will of God for your life. (See Romans 12:1–2.)

THE MAXIMUM MANIFESTATION

One of the most stimulating passages about the call of God is found in the New Testament:

> Brethren, I count not myself to have apprehended: but this one thing I do, forgetting those things which are behind, and reaching forth unto those things which are before, I press toward the mark for the prize of the high calling of God in Christ Jesus.
> —PHILIPPIANS 3:13–14, KJV

Most likely the "high calling" is the maximum manifestation of a believer's potential: not thirtyfold, not sixtyfold, but a hundredfold fulfillment of the divine design. Usually in order to arrive at such a lofty goal, to a certain degree, a person has to forget "those things which are behind" (both the good and the bad). Dwelling on "good" things can lull us into a complacent self-satisfaction; dwelling on "bad" things can overwhelm us with regret, depression, and guilt. So we have to leave these things in the valley below if we are to ascend unhampered to the mountain peak that calls to us from above.

It helps to know that "the gifts and calling of God are irrevocable" (Rom. 11:29). In other words, God normally does not change His mind. Even if His people back off from their purpose, becoming rebellious, cold, indifferent, or simply discouraged, once they repent and renew their commitment, the calling normally emerges once again, for God is faithful.

So let us make our "calling and election sure" (2 Pet. 1:10). That is accomplished by adding to our faith these qualities: virtue, knowledge, self-control, patient endurance, godliness, brotherly kindness, and love. If these things are in us and abound, the Scripture promises that we will not be barren or unfruitful spiritually, and that we will never stumble. (See 2 Peter 1:5–10.)

Let us also "walk worthy of the calling" with which we have been called (Eph. 4:1). Let us shun competition and reach for unity whenever it is possible, for there is only "one hope of our calling"—one ultimate goal that all our callings are ultimately working toward—and that is the full establishment of the kingdom of God on earth at the coming of our Lord Jesus Christ, and our perfection and glorification in Him (Eph. 4:4).

DECLARE WHO YOU ARE IN CHRIST

I declare that I am one of the called! I was given a purpose in the Lord Jesus before the time began and assigned a sufficient amount of grace, power, and gifts to fulfill that purpose. No weapon formed against me shall prosper. All things will work together for my good. My highest calling is to be conformed to the image of the firstborn Son of God. Everything I go through in life—the good and the bad—will work toward this ultimate goal. In great gratitude I have determined to "walk worthy" of the calling and to reach for the "mark of the prize of the high calling of God"—the maximum manifestation of my potential in Christ. In Jesus's name, amen!

Additional reading: 1 Corinthians 1:26–29; 2 Thessalonians 1:10–12; Hebrews 3:1 (NKJV); Revelation 17:14

Chapter 23

THE CHURCH

And the Lord added to *the church* daily
those who were being saved.
—ACTS 2:47

FROM THE VERY start the church was revealed as a work of God, not a work of man. *"The Lord added to the church daily"* by the preaching of the Word and the drawing of the Holy Spirit.

The word "church" is translated from the Greek *ekklésia* (pronounced ek-klay-see'-ah), and it means called out ones. So all who have truly responded to God's calling to come "out of darkness into His marvelous light" are included in its membership (1 Pet. 2:9).

Ekklésia is found 114 times in Scripture according to Englishman's Concordance. In the King James Version it is translated as "assembly" three times (Acts 19:32, 39, 41); all other times it is rendered "church" or "churches." It can refer to the entire church (Matt. 16:18) or to local assemblies (Rev. 1:11). Though the English word *church* is not found in the Old Testament, Stephen, the first martyr of the new covenant, preached about the Israelites on their journey to the Promised Land, and he called them "the church [*ekklésia*] in the wilderness" (Acts 7:38, KJV). So Israel was God's "called out" assembly, called out of the bondage of Egypt into an inherited land and a purpose. In a similar way we of the new covenant can also claim being "the church in the wilderness," for we are all passing through a spiritual wilderness of sin with all of its temptations and challenges, on our journey to the personal promised land of our God-given destiny.[1]

THE PROFESSING CHURCH
VERSUS THE POSSESSING CHURCH

Presently there are over two billion people who claim the Christian faith in this world. Spiritually speaking, there are two primary groups, one contained within the other. First, there is the larger "professing church" who *profess* faith in a historical Christ. Second, there is a smaller-in-number core group that can be labeled the "possessing church," made up of those who actually *possess* a genuine relationship with the Lord Jesus and who have experienced spiritual rebirth. (See John 3:1–7.) This latter group is the true church. They are not signified by any certain denomination but can be found in many different Bible-affirming organizations. They are true lovers of God and have experienced New Testament salvation as it was meant to be. Jesus is not just a religious concept in their minds, for He dwells in their hearts "through faith" (Eph. 3:17).

THE MOST VALUABLE
INSTITUTION IN THE WORLD

Acts 20:28 declares that these born-again individuals make up "the church of God which He purchased with His own blood." Whenever a buyer purchases goods, he must first be convinced that the items of merchandise offered are more valuable to him than the price demanded or the transaction will never take place. In like manner God must have decided that even though we were sin stained, under a curse, and dominated by Satan, we were more valuable to Him than His own blood. What an amazing proof of His great love toward us! Of course, now that its members are truly saved by new covenant standards, the church of God is extremely valuable to His cause, being "the pillar and foundation of the truth" in this world (1 Tim. 3:15).[2]

THE MOST BLESSED
INSTITUTION IN THE WORLD

The Savior asked the disciples an important question about His identity:

> "What do people say about the Son of Man?" The disciples answered, "Some people say you are John the Baptist or maybe Elijah or Jeremiah or some other prophet." Then Jesus asked them, "But who do you say I am?" Simon Peter spoke up, "You are the Messiah, the Son of the living God."
> —MATTHEW 16:13–16, CEV

The conversation continued, detailing the plans and calling Peter had on his life: "Jesus answered and said to him, 'Blessed are you, Simon Bar-Jonah, for flesh and blood has not revealed this to you, but My Father who is in heaven'" (Matt 16:17, NKJV). Then, after giving Simon the name Peter (from the Greek word *petros*, meaning rock), Jesus added: "On this rock I will build *My church*, and the gates of Hades shall not prevail against it" (Matt. 16:18, NKJV).

Hades is the Greek word for the underworld, which in the Old Testament era was the realm of both the wicked and the righteous, separated spiritually by a "great gulf" (Luke 16:26). Of course, in the new covenant that has changed radically. Because Jesus paid the price for our sins to be washed away, we go directly to "the third heaven" ("paradise") at death (2 Cor. 12:2–4). For the Scripture declares, "To be absent from the body" is to be "present with the Lord" (2 Cor. 5:8). So the greatest adversaries of the human race— the curses of death, the grave, and eternal destruction—have not prevailed and will not prevail against the church of the living God. For it has been formed, not by intellectual persuasion, but by super-natural revelation and impartation. Therefore, nothing—absolutely nothing—can separate its members from the One who has opened their eyes to His reality. So quite possibly "the rock" that the church was built on in the beginning (and today as well) is not only Peter's anointed leadership, but also the very thing that convinced Peter that Jesus was truly the Messiah: divine revelation. Because if the Father Himself reveals the Messiah-ship of Jesus to you, no one can shake you from that understanding.

THE MOST PRIVILEGED AND HOLY
INSTITUTION IN THE WORLD

In Ephesians 5:22–33 Paul compares the church to a wife, married to the Lord of glory Himself who "nourishes" and "cherishes" her. Then the apostle reaches all the way back to Eden and likens the union between this bridal church and her heavenly Bridegroom to that first marital union. As Adam said of Eve, "For this reason a man shall leave his father and mother and shall be joined to his wife, and the two shall be one flesh," so Paul says of the church, "we are members of His body, of His flesh and of His bones" (Eph. 5:30–31). Then he revealed: "This is a great mystery, but I am speaking about Christ and the church" (Eph. 5:32).

So we are utterly one with the King of creation. He rejoices to dwell within those who are "married...to Him who has been raised from the dead, so that we may bear fruit for God" (Rom. 7:4). By the impartation of His own nature, He has removed our uncleanness and made us clean and pure in His sight. Thus, when He returns, He will present unto Himself "a glorious church, not having spot, or wrinkle, or any such thing, but that it should be holy and without blemish" (Eph. 5:27).

What an expression of love! No religion in this world can provide such a miracle of transformation! For all eternity we will be the "called out ones"—called out of spiritual contamination into holiness, called out of despair into unutterable joy, called out of a cursed and hopeless state into absolute blessedness and endless hope.

To these things we are compelled to shout out loudly, "Yes, and amen!"

DECLARE WHO YOU ARE IN CHRIST

I declare that I am a member of the true church—the called out ones! I have been born again. I possess a personal relationship with the Savior. I have been called out of bondage into liberty, out of sin into righteousness, out of depression into joy, out of defeat into victory, out of darkness into God's marvelous light. Because I know by revelation that Jesus is the Messiah, the gates of Hades will never prevail against me. Death is already a conquered foe. One day, along with the rest of the church, I will emerge in the resurrection utterly holy and without blemish, victorious over all things forevermore. In Jesus's name, amen!

Additional reading: 1 Corinthians 1:2; Ephesians 1:20–23; 3:9–11, 20–21; Colossians 1:18; Hebrews 12:22–24

Chapter 24

THE CONTRITE ONES

*For thus says the High and Lofty One who inhabits
eternity, whose name is Holy: "I dwell in the high
and holy place, with him who has a contrite and
humble spirit, to revive the spirit of the humble,
and to revive the heart of* the contrite ones.*"*
—ISAIAH 57:15, NKJV

C ONTRITION AND REPENTANCE are inseparably intertwined.
One cannot be truly experienced without the other:

+ Contrition is godly sorrow that causes a change of mind.
+ Repentance is a change of mind that results from godly
  sorrow.

Those who yield to this dual influence turn away from sinful,
earthly things and incline their hearts toward holy, heavenly things.
The Most High responds by communing with such yielded persons in "the high and holy place," lifting them in His Spirit to that
spiritual realm where His power brings transformation (Isa. 57:15).
Those who are privileged to access this "secret place of the Most High"
are spiritually revived (restored to life) as they express love and worship toward the Creator (Ps. 91:1, KJV). They are delivered from the
death-dealing effects of all the negative things faced here below and
renewed by the enlivening power of God's Word and God's Spirit.

Regardless of how grievously a person has erred in life, there is
always hope for restoration. In his early years David experienced the
heights of the beauty of God, yet later in life, he plunged to the ugly
depths of evil. He could have wallowed there in the muck and mire
the remainder of his days, but instead, he mustered the courage and
the tenacity to crawl out and declare with hope: "A broken and a
contrite heart, O God, You will not despise" (Ps. 51:17).

God promises those who maintain this mind-set two precious things, closeness to Him and salvation (deliverance): "The Lord is near to the broken-hearted, and saves the contrite of spirit" (Ps. 34:18).

Being seized by this attitude is not only essential for our own spiritual depth; contrition in the hearts of many can also wield a collective impact on society as a whole. It has always been the foundation of those spiritual awakenings that have affected whole regions with heaven-sent influence and have, at times, even changed the course of history. In the words of W. Graham Scroggie: "There never has been a spiritual revival which did not begin with an acute sense of sin."[1]

In this post-modern era, so steeped in casual Christianity, how desperately we need contrite ones: men and women who have been smitten with grief over the contamination of their own hearts, but who have climbed out of the ashes of the conviction of sin to boldly take hold of their true identity in God. Such choice individuals are the only catalyst that can truly bring hope and change to a generation that is out of control with unrestrained lust and blatant rebellion against the commandments of God.

God tires of powerless and compromised Christianity. Ornately designed religious buildings do not impress Him. Repetitious rituals and ceremonies do not capture His heart. He is not looking for some high-spired cathedral in which to dwell. Instead, He is searching the world over for people of sincere contrition. He revealed this through the Prophet Isaiah:

> Thus says the LORD: "Heaven is My throne, and earth is My footstool. Where is the house that you will build Me? And where is the place of My rest? For all those things My hand has made, and all those things exist," says the LORD. "But on this one will I look: on him who is poor and of a contrite spirit, and who trembles at My Word."
>
> —ISAIAH 66:1–2, NKJV

Those who yield to contrition are often emboldened, losing their fears and inhibitions. Those who tremble at God's Word do not tremble before men. In bold Pentecost style, like the apostles in the beginning, those who yield to contrition are often found lifting their voices unashamedly, shattering religious strongholds and ushering the world around them into a new day spiritually. (See Acts

1–2.) Brokenness gives birth to strength and power and fruitfulness. Hearts thus emptied of self become sanctified vessels filled with the glory and the strength of God that spills over into a needy world.

This really is the key to revival, both individually and globally—and it can start with each one of us today. As we meditate on this calling to be "contrite ones," let us pray for more than just the understanding of a concept; instead, let us appeal to God for its supernatural reality. As Thomas á Kempis wrote: "I would far rather feel contrition than be able define it."[2]

While he was in England, famed revivalist Dwight Moody heard the British evangelist Henry Varley declare: "The world has yet to see what God can do through a man who is totally yielded to Him."[3]

Gripped by these convicting words, Moody concluded, "By the Grace of God, I will be that man"—but maybe, just maybe, someone reading these words could surpass his commitment and his fruitfulness in the kingdom of God.[4] It all starts with being broken before God—and then connecting with the One who came to "heal the broken-hearted" (Isa. 61:1).

DECLARE WHO YOU ARE IN CHRIST

I declare that I am one of the contrite ones! I have decided to build my life on the foundation of "repentance from dead works" (Heb. 6:1). I throw myself on the rock of ages that my will might be completely broken. I refuse the "sorrow of the world," but confess that "godly sorrow" is pleasing to the One who dwells in the high and holy place (2 Cor. 7:10). I believe He will lift me to that place where He revives "the heart of the contrite ones" (Isa. 57:15). As I sincerely repent of anything in my life that is not yielded completely to God, I believe He will resurrect me spiritually to a place of power, courage, love, and fruitfulness far beyond anything I have attained in the past. In Jesus's name, amen!

Additional reading: Matthew 4:17; Mark 2:17; Luke 15:7; Acts 17:29–31; 2 Corinthians 7:9–11; 2 Peter 3:9

Chapter 25

DISCIPLES

Then Jesus said to the Jews who believed on Him, "If you
continue in My Word, you are My *disciples* indeed. And you
shall know the truth, and the truth shall make you free."
—John 8:31–32, nkjv

Adisciple is someone who accepts and assists in spreading
the doctrines of another. The word *disciple* is the root of the
word *discipline*, so it also implies strict adherence to a revealed code
of godly behavior.

This term appears only once in the King James Version of the
Old Testament. It was actually a prophetic reference to believers
in the coming New Testament era. First, the Messiah is described
as "a sanctuary"—a place of rest, refuge, and protection (Isa. 8:14),
and then the prophecy is given: "Bind up the testimony, seal the law
among My disciples" (Isa. 8:16).

This meant that the Messiah's message would be preserved and
entrusted to His followers and the law would be fulfilled—sealed,
finished, brought to completion—through His life and ministry.
Another translation says: "My message and my teachings are to be
sealed and given to my followers" (Isa. 8:16, cev).

What a charge! What a serious responsibility! No wonder "disciple" is the most dominant new covenant title for the people of
God: found over 269 times in the MEV translation.[1] Surely God
emphasized this calling because He wants His people to emphasize
discipleship in their walk with Him.

True disciples are known by the following characteristics:

+ **Forsaking all**: "So likewise, any of you who does not forsake all that he has cannot be My disciple" (Luke 14:33).
  Forsaking all may or may not be literal. Though some have
  literally given up everything to follow Him, all believers

must be *willing*—to put all that they have and all that they are on an altar of consecration to Him.

+ **Loving everything else less:** "If anyone comes to Me and does not hate his father and mother and wife and children and brothers and sisters, yes, and even his own life, he cannot be My disciple" (Luke 14:26). Jesus was not advocating that we treat loved ones with animosity or contempt. The Greek word translated "hate" is *miseó* (pronounced mis-eh´-o), and it can mean to love less.[2]

+ **Bearing much fruit:** "My Father is glorified by this, that you bear much fruit; so you will be My disciples" (John 15:8). Bearing fruit can mean manifesting the character of God (Gal. 5:22–23), winning souls (John 4:36), laboring for the kingdom (Phil. 1:22), and giving praise to God (Heb. 13:15). Abiding in Christ (abiding in the vine) is necessary for this to happen (John 15:4).

+ **Loving others:** "A new commandment I give to you, that you love one another, even as I have loved you, that you also love one another. By this all men will know that you are My disciples, if you have love for one another" (John 13:34–35). The Greek word translated "love" is *agape*. This is the God kind of love—a love so deep, so unselfish, so full, and so rich it can even be bestowed on enemies.

+ **Continuing in His Word:** "If you continue in My Word, you are My disciples indeed" (John 8:31, MKJV). To "continue in His Word" means to lay hold to every provision, fulfill every mandate, and obey every commandment given to believers in this era (there are 1,050 in the New Testament).[3]

+ **Taking up a cross and following Jesus:** "And whoever does not bear his cross and follow Me cannot be My disciple" (Luke 14:27). To "bear a cross" means following Jesus down the road that leads to Calvary, a place of total death to self for the benefit of others. He often initiated the call to discipleship by presenting the challenge, "Follow Me" (Matt 9:9). This means to imitate His character, submit to His will, repeat His works, proclaim His message, and perpetuate His values in this world.

+ **Receiving power from God:** "And when He had called His twelve disciples to Him, He gave them power over unclean spirits, to cast them out, and to heal all kinds of sickness and all kinds of disease" (Matt 10:1, NKJV). The word translated "power" in this verse is *exousia* (pronounced ex-oo-see'-ah), and it can mean mastery. It has also been translated authority.[4] In another parallel passage, Luke 9:1–2, it says, "He called His twelve disciples together and gave them power and authority over all demons and to cure diseases. And He sent them to preach the kingdom of God and to heal the sick." The word translated "power" in that passage is *dunamis* (pronounced doo'-nam-is), and it means force, and has also been translated "ability."[5] So God gives true disciples both authority and ability to effectively represent Him in this world and to conquer the realm of darkness.

+ **Experiencing persecution:** "The disciple is not above his teacher, nor the servant above his master. It is enough for the disciple that he be like his teacher, and the servant like his master. If they have called the master of the house Beelzebub, how much more will they call those of his household?" (Matt. 10:24–25). *Beelzebub* is a derogatory term for the devil that means either "lord of the flies" or god of the dung.[6] The irony and mystery of the matter is that often those who truly represent God's values and His truth are despised, rejected, and persecuted by others—cast in a negative role that is quite opposite to what is actually true. How strange it is that the Beatitudes end with the statement, "Blessed are those who are persecuted for righteousness' sake," for that is often what happens (Matt. 5:10). It's the satanically inspired backlash against those who truly go after godly character.

The Challenge

Though many profess Christianity, a much smaller group, in comparison, truly respond to this discipleship call. However, those who do always become history makers and world changers, even if on a small scale. They fulfill the Lord's mandate to be "the salt of the earth" and "the light of the world"—God's agents of change amid a human race desperately in need of His love and power (Matt. 5:13–14).

Will you dare to accept this discipleship challenge today?

Declare Who You Are in Christ

I declare that I am a disciple of Jesus Christ! My primary goal is to be a disciplined follower of the Lord, forsaking everything except that which is the will of God for my life. I dedicate myself wholly to Him. I intend to continue in His Word, to love others with the love of God, to bear a cross, to be crucified with Christ, to love God and His work more than anyone or anything else in life, and to give the Father glory by bearing much fruit for the kingdom of God in this world. By faith I receive the power—the authority and ability—that God gives to those who accept the discipleship call. In Jesus's name, amen!

Additional reading: Mark 10:17–33; Luke 14:26–33; Romans 12:1–2; Galatians 2:20

Chapter 26

THE LIGHT OF THE WORLD

You are the light of the world. A city that
is set on a hill cannot be hidden.
—**MATTHEW 5:14**

JESUS HAD JUST shared the Beatitudes with His closest disciples, challenging them to be poor in spirit, repentant, meek, righteous, merciful, pure-hearted, and passionate about making peace in a strife-filled world. Then He prophesied: "You are *the light of the world*" (Matt. 5:14) because only people of real godly character can fulfill this calling.

Notice He did not say, "You should be" or "You have the potential of being." Rather, He said, "You are the light of the world!"

The disciples had been with Him only a short time, and of course, they not yet been born again, so they could hardly comprehend the largeness of the destiny unfolding before them. If the Messiah had said "You are the light of Jerusalem," it would have been much easier to believe. But He said, "*the world*." I can almost imagine them shaking their heads in amazement as they discussed it later.

How could this be? There were only twelve of them, and they were just common and uneducated men. How could they ever hope to have *worldwide* impact? But the Son of God's words kept echoing within their hearts, causing them to feel the heavy weight of a sacred charge. A desperately needy world, writhing in darkness, was pleading for their help. At that point they must not have felt very capable of making a difference. All they knew to do was to keep following Jesus, watch the light shine through Him, and then do it like He did.

THE ADULTEROUS WOMAN

Not long after His Beatitude message, Jesus demonstrated how to be "light of the world" on two separate occasions.

The first time, an angry mob of Jews threw a distressed, disheveled woman at Jesus's feet claiming she had just been caught in the act of adultery. (I've always wondered what happened to the man.) They were strict legalists—fiercely religious people. Like a pack of predator wolves, they prowled around Israel, ready to pounce on the weak and the erring. They were quite the opposite of true religion—don't you agree?

Jesus knelt down next to her trembling frame, feeling her pain and remorse. He wrote on the ground. Then the same voice that said, "Let there be light" in the beginning "separated the light from the darkness" once again by saying, "Let him who is without sin among you be the first to throw a stone at her" (Gen. 1:3–4; John 8:7).

The darkness of pride, anger, and judgmental, hyper-religious attitudes had to flee. The light of love, righteousness, and truth shone forth as He said—"Neither do I condemn you. Go and sin no more" (John 8:11). Then that choice, defining moment arrived. He gazed at the stymied onlookers and boldly announced:

> I am *the light of the world*. Whoever follows Me shall not walk
> in the darkness, but shall have the light of life.
>
> —JOHN 8:12

What a magnificent confession! As the light of heaven spilled over into the physical world, it illuminated the consciences of the stone-throwers with a revelation of the mercy of God. It flooded the hearts of the disciples with courage, proving the power of love. It radiated hope to a broken woman in deep despair. Yes, all were enlightened by the experience. And the light that emanated from that single event on the Mount of Olives is shining still—nearly two thousand years later—illuminating an angry, gloomy, guilt-ridden, and religion-filled world with the kindness of God.

THE MAN BORN BLIND

In the very next chapter Jesus passed by a man blind from birth. As if on que, His disciples asked, "Rabbi, who sinned, this man or his parents, that he was born blind?" (John 9:2). Jesus responded: "Neither this man nor his parents sinned. But it happened so that the works of God might be displayed in him" (John 9:3).

In one short sentence the Messiah shined eternal light on a question that has always plagued the minds of men—the reason for human suffering. Though this is not always the case, it often provides an opportunity for God to reveal His character as He intervenes in painful circumstances. (In fact, the sum total of all the pain wracking the human race merely set the stage for Calvary, which revealed the love of God in the greatest degree possible—globally.) Then Jesus proclaimed:

> While I am in the world, I am *the light of the world.*
>
> —John 9:5

After spitting on the ground and making some muddy paste, He anointed the blind man's eyes, instructing him to go wash in the pool of Siloam. The miracle happened! But it caused a whirlwind of opposition because Jesus dared to do it on the Sabbath. The prideful Pharisees were so blinded by their own religious tradition, they could not even see the glory of God moving in their midst. (I still shake my head with amazement—is that not beyond belief?) No wonder John, in the beginning of his Gospel, said the light shined in the darkness, but "the darkness did not comprehend it" (John 1:5, NKJV). All they could see was Jesus's disregard for their tradition. But the meek saw their lives light up with the power and the influence of the truth.

Remember Jesus qualified this calling with the words, "*While I am in the world,* I am the light of the world." But He left after thirty-three and a half years, ascending back to His heavenly throne. That's when He passed the torch to His people. The light did not stop shining then. Quite the contrary, instead of illuminating the darkness in one place, at one time, the blazing inward torch multiplied exponentially and began radiating in thousands of places from thousands of sources.

Now in these latter days—the closing of the church era—it is imperative that without hesitancy we assume this responsibility. The war is on; the prince of darkness is pursuing his diabolical plan to capture the final generation in a web of dark deception with the bait of self-indulgence. But God has a greater plan, revealed nearly three thousand years ago through the Prophet Isaiah. To the elect remnant of the closing era, God commands:

> Arise, shine, for your light has come, and the glory of the LORD has risen upon you. For the darkness shall cover the earth and deep darkness the peoples; but the LORD shall rise upon you, and His glory shall be seen upon you.
>
> —ISAIAH 60:1–2

This is our day! A day of glory! We must refuse to be intimidated by the darkness. Let the darkness be intimidated by us. It's time to arise and shine!

DECLARE WHO YOU ARE IN CHRIST

I declare that I am a part of a body of believers called to be the light of the world! I refuse for darkness to have any control over my thoughts, my emotions, my words or my actions. I know that I can only be the light if I "walk in the light as He is in the light" (1 John 1:7). So I choose to yield to the brightness of God's character: His love, forgiveness, mercy, righteousness, and goodness. By yielding to and manifesting His nature, I am driving back the darkness in my sphere of influence. Moreover, the Lord of light is using me to advance His kingdom of light in this world. In Jesus's name, amen!

Additional reading: Psalm 27:1; Isaiah 9:2; Matthew 5:16; John 1:1–9 (NKJV), 1 John 1:5–7; Revelation 21:23–24; 22:5

Chapter 27

THE PURE IN HEART

Blessed are the pure in heart, for they shall see God.
—MATTHEW 5:8

THIS IS THE sixth beatitude in Jesus's famed Sermon on the Mount. A careful reading of the first five shows progressive steps that lead to this goal of purity of heart:

+ *"Blessed are the poor in spirit"*—first, we admit our spiritual bankruptcy in Adam (Matt. 5:3).

+ *"Blessed are those who mourn"*—second, we grieve over the fallen nature and our personal failings (Matt. 5:4).

+ *"Blessed are the meek"*—third, we humbly submit to God's rule in our lives (Matt. 5:5).

+ *"Blessed are those who hunger and thirst for righteousness"*—fourth, we long to live a life in conformity with God's commandments (Matt. 5:6).

+ *"Blessed are the merciful"*—fifth, we show compassion toward those who struggle with sin, who are needy in many ways (Matt. 5:7).

Then we arrive at purity of heart. So the first milestone on the road to purity is admitting that within ourselves we are not pure and the last stretch in the road involves showing love and patience toward others who do not yet measure up.

GOD IS THE ABSOLUTE OF PURITY

To God, Habakkuk acknowledged, "You are pure and cannot stand the sight of evil" (Hab. 1:13, NLT; see also James 1:13). In light of this it seems impossible that any member of this fallen human race could ever truly have fellowship with God. The Book of Job even presents the question:

> How then can man be justified and righteous before God? Or how can he who is born of a woman be pure and clean? Behold, even the moon has no brightness [compared to God's glory] and the stars are not pure in His sight—how much less man, who is a maggot! And a son of man, who is a worm!
>
> —JOB 25:4–6, AMPC

What a predicament! Is there a solution? Step one is identifying what makes us impure and then dealing with it. Under the old covenant many things were classified as sources of impurity and elaborate rituals were prescribed to remedy the condition. An important one involved something called the "water of purification" (Num. 19:9). It was made from the ashes of a red heifer burned outside the camp of Israel. The ashes were mixed with running water and sprinkled on those who needed to be cleansed.

Numbers 19 lists some of the conditions that made it necessary for Jews to participate in this ritual: touching a corpse or just being in a room when someone died, touching a bone, touching a grave, or just touching a person who was unclean because of contact with these things. So associating with death in any way rendered a person impure. If not remedied, such defiled persons could be cut off from Israel.

Though we are not subject to these demands now, they still speak to us in symbolic, prophetic ways.

First, Adam and Eve "touched death" in the beginning and they transferred this state of death to all of us—spiritual death, emotional death, mental death, physical death, and ultimately the "second death" (Rev. 21:8). In like manner, naturally speaking, we pass death to our offspring.

Second, in this broken world we are constantly in contact with death-dealing influences:

+ "For the wages of sin is death" (Rom. 6:23).
+ "To be carnally minded is death" (Rom. 8:6).

- "He who does not love his brother abides in death" (1 John 3:14, NKJV).

By these things we touch death and become impure in God's sight. O God, help us! Our dilemma is great! How can we recover? Hebrews gives the welcome answer:

> For if the blood of bulls and goats, and the ashes of a heifer, sprinkling the unclean, sanctifies so that the flesh is purified, how much more shall the blood of Christ, who through the eternal Spirit offered Himself without blemish to God, cleanse your conscience from dead works to serve the living God?
> —HEBREWS 9:13–14

The ashes of a heifer only offered an external, temporary fix. The blood of Jesus grants us an internal and eternal transformation. In the first apostolic council Peter explained how the Gentile household of Cornelius had received salvation and though they were not Jews, God—"made no distinction between them and us, and *purified their hearts by faith*" (Acts 15:9).

So in the new covenant Jesus responds to our faith by giving us a pure heart *supernaturally* so that we can walk in purity *naturally*. Internal purity (that comes as a gift) should automatically result in external purity (that is the result of continued consecration on our part).

This is all building toward that final day when purity will be exalted to its highest degree:

> Beloved, now are we children of God, and it has not yet been revealed what we shall be. But we know that when He appears, we shall be like Him, for we shall see Him as He is. *Everyone who has this hope in Him purifies himself, just as He is pure.*
> —1 JOHN 3:2–3

According to this passage as we look forward to the resurrection from the dead, there is an overflow of purifying power into our hearts—right here, right now—until we are glorified and eventually become just as pure as the One who gave us this hope-filled promise. Then, when He returns to fully establish His kingdom, we will "see Him" in all of His radiant glory. On that grand day the divine pledge will reach its highest degree of fulfillment:

> Blessed are the pure in heart, for they shall see God.
> —MATTHEW 5:8

We can only imagine how spectacular that moment of unveiling will be!

DECLARE WHO YOU ARE IN CHRIST

I declare that I am called to be one of the pure in heart! I acknowledge this is only possible by divine intervention. According to Titus 2:14 Jesus came to this world to "purify for Himself a special people." I choose to cooperate with God in this process by loving Him with all my heart and doing my utmost to obey the truth. In so doing, I believe I will see God moving supernaturally in my life right here, right now, and I will also see God in all of His glory in the world to come. In Jesus's name, amen!

Additional reading: Psalm 12:6; Philippians 4:8; 1 Timothy 3:9 (NKJV); Hebrews 9:22–26; 10:22; James 4:8; 1 Peter 1:22

Chapter 28

THE SALT OF THE EARTH

*You are the salt of the earth; but if the salt loses its flavor,
how shall it be seasoned? It is then good for nothing
but to be thrown out and trampled underfoot by men.*
—MATTHEW 5:13, NKJV

SALT IS A substance purposefully used to change whatever it
contacts. So when Jesus told His disciples, "You are the salt of
the earth," in essence He was saying, "You are God's chosen catalyst
to bring change to this world."

When the world changes the church it's called apostasy. But when
the church changes the world—that's true revival. When it happens,
it's an indication that believers have truly accepted this challenge
to be salt. Jesus was a living example of someone who fulfilled this
calling, because when He came to the earth, major shifts took place
that changed the world forever.

Unfortunately many believers do not have a "salt" mind-set;
instead, they barely function in a "survival" mode—striving to
implement enough biblical truth just to survive the battles of life.
But God has called His people to be proactive, not just reactive. We
are His agents of transformation in a world that desperately needs it.

EXPANDING THE REVELATION

Quite often the Bible defines its own symbols, and such is the case
with salt. Colossians 4:6 commands: "Let your speech always be
with grace, seasoned with salt."

So according to this passage salt represents grace. First, God salts
us with grace, changing our hearts and lives, then He salts the world
with grace-filled believers who utter grace-filled words to change
others. Other translations of this verse say that our words should be
"gracious" (ISV), "pleasant and interesting" (GNT), and "kind and well

thought out" (GW). In other words, the most influential believers are those who have overcome the religious tendency of becoming harsh, judgmental rule givers, and have instead wisely reached out to the world as forgiving, compassionate grace givers.

There are at least four other attributes of salt that symbolize various roles that we should passionately fill as true disciples of the Lord Jesus:

+ **Salt is a flavor enhancer.** Often we use salt to enhance the flavor of food, making bland or even bitter food enjoyable. So believers who fulfill this salt calling are used by God to enhance the flavor of life for those who are enduring a bland or even bitter existence. The world is full of people who face deep depression, anxiety, fear, or despair. God sends His salty people into their lives to make an otherwise inedible meal a feast of hope, joy, peace, forgiveness, and love.

+ **Salt is an antiseptic.** Salt has germ-killing properties; it can halt the progress of infections. So those who fulfill the calling to be the salt of the earth often put a stop to the contagious disease of sin in the environment around them. By introducing godly values and the knowledge of salvation into their world, they provide the antidote for souls made sick by the carnality and sensuality that prevails here.

+ **Salt is a preservative.** Especially before the advent of refrigerators, salt was used to keep meat from rotting. It is still added to many types of foods as a preservative. So those who fulfill this calling are used of God to preserve biblical truth and godly values in a society that often rejects such standards.

+ **Salt is a cleansing or purifying agent.** Salt is made of two primary elements: sodium and chloride. When taken through electrolysis (being submerged in water and subjected to an electric current) salt is broken down into its two parts. Both remaining substances are used as cleansing agents: sodium is employed to make soap, and chloride is used for the purpose of whitening or purifying other things. So it is, when God's people are submerged in the water of the Word and His power flows through their lives, the end result is brokenness before Him. When this truly transpires, such yielded sons and daughters of God become His salt-like cleansing agents—for by their influence, sin-stained persons are washed and purified, and their spiritual garments are made white.

In Luke 14:33 Jesus informed those who heard Him that they must "forsake all" to be His disciples, then He continued with the statement: "Salt is good; but if the salt has lost its flavor, how shall it be seasoned?" (Luke 14:34, NKJV). So we can conclude that the flavor of a true disciple is complete self-sacrifice, forsaking the reigns of control over all our decisions to follow the perfect will of God.

Teddy Roosevelt, a former president of the United States, once used this salt symbol to encourage others to live self-sacrificing lives. He declared:

> No man is worth his salt who is not ready at all times to risk his well-being, to risk his body, to risk his life, in a great cause.[1]

What did he mean by the phrase *"worth his salt"*? It's a cliché stemming from the ancient practice of Roman soldiers being paid sometimes with salt instead of money. The original Latin word is *salarium*, from which we get our modern word *salary*.[2] So back then if you were a loyal, disciplined, strong, fierce fighter on the battlefield, you were *"worth your salt."* Changing Teddy Roosevelt's quote slightly, we could say:

> No Christian is worth the application of God's grace to his life (no believer is worth his salt) unless he is willing to passionately and courageously sacrifice his life for the supreme cause of all—the proclamation of the gospel and the advance of the kingdom of God.

Three things are very salty in the human body: blood, sweat, and tears. So Christians who truly fulfill this mandate will often be discovered weeping for what they believe, working for what they believe, and if necessary, even dying for what they believe. Considering this and all the other points made in this chapter, can we truthfully say that we are measuring up to this high standard of being "the salt of the earth"? It might be a good time to pray right now.

DECLARE WHO YOU ARE IN CHRIST

I declare that I, along with the rest of the body of Christ, am called to be the salt of the earth! I embrace this purpose in all of its facets. I make a commitment to enhance the flavor of life for those who have a bland or bitter existence to endure. I choose to arrest the progress of sin and corruption in the lives of people around me. I am determined to preserve godly values in an often ungodly culture, and I choose to be broken and clean before God that He might use me to cleanse the hearts of others. Finally I forsake all— everything I have and everything I am, I now place under the lordship of Jesus Christ—for this is the "salty flavor" of true discipleship. Let it be so. In Jesus's name, amen!

Additional reading: Leviticus 2:13; 2 Chronicles 13:1–5; Job 6:6; Mark 9:41–50; Luke 14:25–35

Chapter 29

TRUE WORSHIPPERS

Yet the hour is coming, and is now here, when the
true worshippers will worship the Father in spirit and
truth. For the Father seeks such to worship Him.
—JOHN 4:23

THIS WORLD IS a place of seeking, a place where thirsty people seek after the Father and where the Father seeks to find thirsty people—"true worshippers" who are able to fulfill His desire for sweet communion and meaningful relationship.

For this very reason the Son of God came to earth: "to seek and to save that which was lost" (Luke 19:10). Being of that mindset, He initiated a conversation with a lowly woman near a well in Samaria—someone His followers would have overlooked entirely— but He saw a deep well of desire for truth in her heart.

He began with the simple request, *"Give Me to drink"* (John 4:7, KJV). Surprised that a Jew would even speak to a Samaritan, her eyes mirrored wonder. If she had only known the irony of His statement. For "all things were created by Him" (Col. 1:16), and that includes the Atlantic, Pacific, Indian, Arctic, and Antarctic oceans. All these huge bodies of water came forth from Him, as well as every river, lake, pond, and drop of rain that falls from the sky. So He really didn't need her little bucket of water. He could have effortlessly brought forth His own source. But He wanted to see her willingness and the response of her heart, so He continued:

> Jesus answered her, "If you knew the gift of God, and who it is who is saying to you, 'Give Me a drink,' you would have asked Him, and He would have given you living water....Everyone who drinks of this water will thirst again, but whoever drinks of the water that I shall give him will never thirst. Indeed, the

> water that I shall give him will become in him a well of water
> springing up into eternal life."
>
> —John 4:10, 13–14

Ponder this wording carefully. This "living water" first flows *into us* to quench our thirst, then it flows *out of us*. This river of love streams from God's throne into our hearts to heal us, only to return to Him as a fountain of love and gratitude.

But what really is this "living water"? Natural water—H_2O, a staple of life—is made up of two elements: two parts hydrogen and one part oxygen. "Living water," an even more important staple of life, is also made of two spiritual elements. Biblically, water represents both the Word (see Isaiah 55:10–11; Ephesians 5:26) and the Spirit (see John 7:37–39). Fusing these two symbols together, therefore, "living water" could easily be described as $WORD_2SPIRIT$: two parts Word (Old Testament and New Testament) and one part Spirit. By these two things God quenches our thirst for spiritual reality—both of which stream back to Him when we worship. Jesus revealed this to the woman at the well when He said: "God is Spirit, and those who worship Him must worship in spirit and truth" (John 4:24).

Our hearts (full of His Spirit) and our minds (full of His truth) respond in adoration.

But let's go a little deeper and discover what this dual requirement really means.

Worshipping "in Spirit"

Notice the word *spirit* is spelled with a lowercase s in John 4:24. So it is not referring to God's Spirit, but rather, the regenerated spirit of a born-again believer. Until Jesus dwells within, our spirits are "dead in…trespasses and sins" (Eph. 2:1). Even though the spirit has a three-fold function (communion with God, revelation from God, and conscience), the first two are nonfunctional prior to salvation. The third (conscience) is defiled and barely functional. But at the moment of spiritual rebirth, God puts a "new spirit" (Ezek. 11:19) in us that is "created according to God in righteousness and true holiness" (Eph. 4:24). This new spirit, or the "new creation" in Christ (2 Cor. 5:17, NKJV), has the capacity of offering true worship to God and receiving true revelation from Him. The conscience also is cleansed "to serve the living God" (Heb 9:14). In other words, a new sensitivity to what pleases God is given so a believer can live a life of worshipful obedience. No other religion can offer its adherents this miraculous internal restoration.

WORSHIPPING "IN TRUTH"

There are seven primary ways that we "worship in truth":

1. Worshipping with honesty—acknowledging sin (See Psalm 51:3.)

2. Worshipping with sincerity—with the whole heart (See Psalm 9:1.)

3. Worshipping with the right revelation of the nature of God (See Exodus 34:14; John 4:22.)

4. Worshipping with correct methods (See Psalms 47:1; 100:1–5; Lamentations 3:41.)

5. Worshipping by learning and comprehending the truth (See 2 Timothy 2:15.)

6. Worshipping by applying that truth to every area of our lives (See Psalm 86:11–12.)

7. Worshipping "in Christ"—abiding in the One who said, "I am…the truth" (John 14:6)

Other translations of our highlighted verse, John 4:23, refer to these kind of people as "real worshippers" (NEB) or "genuine worshipers" (BER). Of all goals in life, this is one of the most important—to be real, to be genuine with the almighty God, rather than just religious, to be lovers of God. As Isaac Watts penned: "Let every act of worship be, like our espousals, Lord, to thee."[1]

Oh, by the way, God doesn't really need our buckets of worship either since He is surrounded by an "ocean of devotion," a multitude of angels that ceaselessly praise His name. But He is still saying to each one of us individually, "*Give Me to drink.*" He still wants to see our willingness and He wants to sense the response of our hearts. Pour out your heart to Him today!

Declare Who You Are in Christ

I declare that I am called to be a true worshipper! I approach God with no ulterior motives or hidden agenda in seeking Him. I am not in love with religion; I am in love with God. I don't seek God to get; I seek God to give—of myself entirely. My prayer is that everything I say and do breathes worship the Lord's direction, so that my life is in constant communion with Him. I make a commitment to always worship God "in spirit and truth"—worshipping Him with all honesty and sincerity. I acknowledge that it is only in Christ that I have access to the Almighty, so I bow before Him adoringly with great gratitude for accepting me into His holy presence. In Jesus's name, amen!

Additional reading: Psalm 29:1–2 (NKJV); Matthew 4:8–10; John 9:31; Revelation 4:10–11

PART 5

YOU ARE
EMPOWERED

Chapter 30

AMBASSADORS FOR CHRIST

Now then, we are *ambassadors for Christ*, as though
God were pleading through us: we implore you
on Christ's behalf, be reconciled to God.
—2 CORINTHIANS 5:20, NKJV

AN AMBASSADOR IS a representative, a messenger, or one sent on a specific errand.

The person who effectively fills this role seeks to speak not his own mind but the mind of the leader or the nation he represents. Therefore, an ambassador is someone who has lost his own personal agenda, assuming the identity and heralding the cause of another.

John the Baptist was truly one of heaven's greatest ambassadors. When he was asked by his detractors to identify himself, he could have easily boasted, "I am the son of Zechariah, the high priest, the sole heir of the most respected religious position in Israel." Instead he responded, "I am the voice of one crying out in the wilderness, 'Make straight the way of the Lord'" (John 1:23; see also Isaiah 40:3; Malachi 3:1). When this last of all the Old Testament prophets walked across the pages of history, he was not striving to draw attention to himself. On the contrary, his mission and message were far more important than his own person, and his passion was exalting the Messiah. He even declared, "He must increase, but I must decrease" (John 3:30).

So the first dominant character trait of a true ambassador is *selflessness*.

When a United States ambassador speaks, it is understood that he is sanctioned and supported by all the combined authority of the US Army, Navy, Marines, Air Force, Coast Guard, Pentagon, the infrastructure of all law enforcement and government agencies, Congress, Senate, and all the way up to the president himself. It's as if an invisible host of supportive onlookers surround the ambassador and lend their united influence and superior strength, even in hostile and challenging areas of the world. It is no wonder that an ambassador can stave off a major war or sway a whole nation, for he or she could well say, "There are more for me than there are against me."

In like manner, as "ambassadors of the Messiah" (2 Cor. 5:20, CJB), we are encompassed with a "great cloud of witnesses" (Heb 12:1), for not only do we speak in the name of the King of all kings, we also represent the entire kingdom and all its citizenry. Our authority is undergirded by all God's chosen under the old covenant, including the patriarchs, prophets, judges, priests, and all of Israel, as well as all of God's people under the new covenant: the entire body of Christ spanning two millennia. When we speak under the direction of God and under His anointing, what we say can potentially bear just as much authority as the Lord of hosts speaking Himself, who sends armies of angels to execute His Word when it is truly spoken through us.

So ambassadors are also persons of great *authority* who can act with great *boldness*!

Jesus was the primary ambassador of heaven, the best example of this calling to all who would ever follow. All believers are chosen to walk in His likeness—continuing His mission and perpetuating His message. It is not a message of condemnation or religious legalism, or a curse. Quite the contrary, it is a message of love, mercy, forgiveness, and restoration. No wonder it is called "the gospel" (meaning good news).

Look at our main verse again in its context:

> All this is from God, who has reconciled us to Himself through Jesus Christ and has given to us *the ministry of reconciliation*, that is, that God was in Christ reconciling the world to Himself, not counting their sins against them, and has entrusted to us *the message of reconciliation*. So we are *ambassadors for Christ*, as though God were pleading through us. We implore you in Christ's stead: *Be reconciled to God*. God made Him who knew no sin to be sin for us, that we might become the righteousness of God in Him.
>
> —2 CORINTHIANS 5:18–21

Ambassadors of heaven are called to be God's mouthpieces, equipped with the principal ministry and message of the firstborn Son—which, according to this passage, is reconciliation (restoration to a right and harmonious relationship with God). In this new covenant era especially God is not interested in *cutting people off*. On the contrary, He is very passionate about *cutting people free* from the sin of their past and the judgment they should all receive.

So instead of going through life poised to condemn others for their bad actions and attitudes, whenever possible let's rightly represent heaven by declaring the incredible power of the cross—the Messiah's promise to restore even the most erring yet repentant human beings to a harmonious, peaceful, and fruitful relationship with the Father above.

Remember, an ambassador normally resides in an embassy. The flag of the nation he represents flies above the compound even if it is located in a nation that is politically quite different. If the host country is a place of dictatorial or communistic rule, but the ambassador is from a free democracy—his or her embassy serves as an oasis of freedom in the midst of a place of suffocating societal bondage. In like manner, the homes of believers are heaven's embassies, each one an oasis of freedom and eternal life in a world full of the horrifying bondage of sin and death. So fly the gospel flag high over your life! Every day you are offering hope to many.

DECLARE WHO YOU ARE IN CHRIST

I declare that I am an ambassador of Jesus Christ! I make a commitment to do what Jesus would do, say what Jesus would say, and express the attitudes He would manifest—if He were in the same situation with the same people. As a representative of heaven, I dare to assert spiritual authority. I speak for the King of glory. When aligned with His Word, what I say is filled with the power to bring change. Angels have been sent forth to execute God's Word spoken through me. I confess that my main message and my main mission in life is to reconcile erring human beings to God and share with them the "gift of righteousness" that He bought through much suffering and delights to give away (Rom. 5:17). In Jesus's name, amen!

Additional reading: Proverbs 13:17 (NKJV); Romans 5:10; Ephesians 6:20; Colossians 1:21–23

Chapter 31

HIS ANOINTED

The Lord is the strength of His people, and He
is the saving strength of *His anointed*.
—**Psalm 28:8**

T O BE ANOINTED means to be chosen by God and endued with a measure of His Spirit to fulfill an ordained purpose. Our title scripture reveals that God supernaturally strengthens and protects such blessed individuals. Consider a few classic examples: David faced Goliath; Daniel was thrown in the lion's den; and Meshach, Shadrach, and Abednego were cast into the furnace of fire. In all of these cases God was the "saving strength" of His chosen representatives, and by His Spirit they supernaturally overcame impossible situations.

But what about those who were martyred, who lost their lives serving God—such as Stephen, Peter, or Paul? Did something go wrong? No, these consecrated persons fulfilled their appointed time on earth, and when the greatest adversary of all appeared—death—they still emerged victorious. God's "saving strength" enabled them to overcome what no human being can overcome on his own. Instead of death being an end for such anointed ones, it became a portal into a glorious, eternal existence in a spiritual sphere.

Concerning the patriarchs of old, Abraham, Isaac, and Jacob, God forthrightly declared, "Do not touch My anointed ones, and do no harm to my prophets" (Ps. 105:15). As they passed through this world—often shunned, disregarded, opposed, persecuted, or outnumbered—still they were under God's oversight and received His provision and protection. Not only did they survive; they also thrived in what they were sent to accomplish.

Under the old covenant certain choice leaders in seven categories were included among "the anointed": patriarchs, judges, kings, governors, prophets, priests, and in some cases soldiers (those supernaturally empowered in battle). Then the Messiah came (so translated from the Hebrew *mashiyach*, meaning the anointed One).[1] The "oil of gladness" (the supernatural "oil" of the anointing) rested upon Him in an unprecedented, unsurpassed way (Ps. 45:7). Quoting from the Prophet Isaiah's writings (Isa. 61:1–2), He announced His ministry in the synagogue at Nazareth:

> The Spirit of the Lord is upon Me, *because He has anointed Me* to preach the gospel to the poor; He has sent Me to heal the broken-hearted, to preach deliverance to the captives and recovery of sight to the blind, to set at liberty those who are oppressed; to preach the acceptable year of the Lord.
>
> —Luke 4:18–19

He was the epitome, the most excellent expression, of all seven categories of persons anointed under the old covenant—for He was, is, and ever will be the Patriarch of all patriarchs, the "Ancient of Days" Himself (Dan. 7:9); the "Judge of all the earth" (Gen. 18:25); the "KING OF KINGS" (Rev. 19:16); the governor among the nations (Ps. 22:28); the great Prophet that Moses said would come (Deut. 18:15; Acts 3:22); the "great High Priest" (Heb. 4:14); and the exemplary soldier, the "captain of [our] salvation" (Heb. 2:10, kjv). All seven anointed roles were fulfilled to perfection on the highest spiritual level in just one person—also referred to in the New Testament as "the Christ" (from the Greek word *Christos*, meaning the anointed One).

Later on Peter shared "how God anointed Jesus of Nazareth with the Holy Spirit and with power" and that as a result, He "went about doing good and healing all who were oppressed by the devil, for God was with Him" (Acts 10:38). That's probably the most exact, concise way of describing our God-given purpose as well. All true born-again believers are now among "the anointed"; we have all received the indwelling of His Spirit who empowers us to "preach the gospel," "heal the broken-hearted," and go about "doing good."

This may be a dangerous and deception-filled world, but we can have absolute confidence. In his first epistle John encouraged New Testament believers with the following exhortation:

> But the anointing which you have received from Him remains in you, and you do not need anyone to teach you. For as the

same anointing teaches you concerning all things, and is truth, and is no lie, and just as it has taught you, remain in Him.

—1 John 2:27

In this passage three primary promises are given to anointed ones:

+ The anointing will remain in us all our days.
+ The anointing will teach us all things.
+ The anointing will instruct us how to remain or abide in God.

Thank God, these three things will be our "saving strength" until we transcend into the heavenly realm and then progress to the next stage of our destiny in the Lord: reigning with Him as kings and priests on this earth.

Oh, by the way, we will be anointed for that God-ordained task also.

Declare Who You Are in Christ

I declare that I am one of the anointed of the Lord! The anointing of the Holy Spirit, the "oil of gladness," has been placed in my heart and on my life to accomplish a God-given purpose. I am well equipped spiritually to fulfill the perfect will of God. He will be my "saving strength" in every situation. The Messiah was anointed to heal the brokenhearted and to proclaim liberty to the captives. I am anointed for these things also. I declare that God's anointing will abide in me all my days, teach me all things, and instruct me how to abide in Him until I transcend this world to fulfill the next stage of my destiny. In Jesus's name, amen!

Additional reading: 1 Samuel 2:10; Isaiah 10:27 (kjv); Psalms 2:1–9; 92:10; Hebrews 1:8–9; 1 John 2:20

Chapter 32

CHILDREN OF THE COVENANT

You are the *children* of the prophets, and *of the covenant* which God made with our fathers.
—ACTS 3:25, WEB

A COVENANT IS a pact between two or more parties, each binding himself to fulfill certain obligations. From the beginning of time God has progressively revealed His plan for humankind by establishing divinely inspired covenants. The nine most important, foundational covenants are as follows:

+ **The Edenic Covenant:** the covenant of creation, made with Adam and Eve before the fall (See Genesis 1:26–31; 2:7–25.)

+ **The Adamic Covenant:** the covenant of redemption, made with Adam and Eve after the fall (See Genesis 3:7–24.)

+ **The Noahic Covenant:** the covenant of restoration, made with Noah after the flood waters subsided (See Genesis 8:13–9:17.)

+ **The Abrahamic Covenant:** the covenant of blessing, made with Abraham and his offspring (See Genesis 12–22.)

+ **The Mosaic Covenant:** the covenant of law, made with Moses and the children of Israel fifty days out of Egypt at Horeb; most likely, the name of the range that contains Mount Sinai (See Deuteronomy 5:1–5.)

+ **The Promised Land Covenant:** the covenant of conquering, made with Israel in the plains of Moab after forty years in the wilderness in preparation for their entrance into the land of Canaan and possession of their God-given inheritance (See Deuteronomy 29:1–15; 30:19–20.)

- **The Davidic Covenant:** the covenant of mercy, made with David concerning the eternal preservation of his throne and dynasty, which came to pass through the Messiah who descended from him (See 2 Samuel 7; 1 Chronicles 17; Psalms 89; 132; Isaiah 9:6–9; Jeremiah 23:5–6; 33:14–22; Matthew 1:1–17; Luke 3:22–38.)

- **The New Covenant:** made with anyone in this present era, Jew or Gentile, who repents and believes in the Messiah, granting an inner transformation that makes believers "new creations" in Christ and heirs of eternal life (See Jeremiah 31:31–34; 2 Corinthians 3:5–18; 5:17–21; Hebrews 8:1–13.)

- **The Everlasting Covenant:** made up of all those elements of the previous eight covenants that have permanent relevance and eternal application (See Hebrews 13:20.)

There have also been a number of subordinate, complementary covenants authored by God, such as the covenant of sure mercies (Isa. 55:3), the covenant of peace (Isa. 54:10), and the family legacy covenant (Isa. 59:20–21).

Each of the primary covenants has at least three, and usually five main elements:

- **The words of the covenant:** blessings and curses, promises and conditions

- **The sacrifice of the covenant:** the price paid to secure and ratify the covenant, usually a sacrificial animal until the supreme sacrifice was paid on Calvary

- **The token of the covenant:** a visible and symbolic reminder of the invisible pact between God and His people, such as the flaming sword, circumcision, or the rainbow

- **The mediator of the covenant:** the one who receives and proclaims the revelation of the covenant, passing it on to future recipients

- **The place of the covenant:** a sacred location where the covenant is first revealed, ratified, or established

Responding to the Covenant

God is a covenant-making, covenant-revealing, covenant-keeping, and covenant-establishing God. Entering a covenant with Him involves accepting His terms and sincerely reciprocating. That means responding with faith, love, holiness, worshipfulness, fruitfulness, and lifelong commitment. Only then can the covenant be fully functional.

This hallowed commitment is binding—both on God's part and ours. In this era, to every one of His sons and daughters, God promises, "I will never leave you, nor forsake you" (Heb. 13:5). His expectation is for responders to rise up to that same level of commitment by daring to say, "Lord, to the best of my ability, I will never leave you, and I will never forsake you."

How comforting it is to know, if we are in covenant with the Creator, that our burdens and battles are now His! In mutual covenantal fashion, it is also true that His burdens and His battles now belong to us. So what is God's burden? Evidently the salvation of lost humanity. And what are His battles? The conquest of Satan, the reacquisition of this planet, and the full establishment of the kingdom of God in this world. If we claim to be in covenant with God, these visionary goals will necessarily dominate our minds and our lives.

The New Covenant

Every covenant evolves out of those previously revealed. The one in which we are now participating is called "the new covenant" (Matt. 26:28). The words of this covenant are powerful, for God promises to place His Word and His Spirit within the hearts of those who accept His terms of repentance, faith, and surrender to the lordship of Jesus.

During the old covenant being accepted by God depended on keeping the law. This proved too difficult for most participants and insufficient in meeting mankind's primary need. However, the Prophet Jeremiah foretold the dawning of a new day:

> Surely, the days are coming, says the LORD, when I will make
> *a new covenant* with the house of Israel and with the house
> of Judah....I will put My law within them and write it in
> their hearts; and I will be their God, and they shall be My

people....They all shall know Me....I will forgive their iniquity, and I will remember their sin no more.

—Jeremiah 31:31–34

Likewise, the Prophet Ezekiel foretold the new covenant:

Thus says the Lord God...I will give you a new heart, and a new spirit I will put within you....I will put My Spirit within you and cause you to walk in My statutes.

—Ezekiel 36:22, 26–27

This dual promise of the new covenant (the indwelling Word and Spirit of God) has brought reconciliation, restoration, and transformation to multitudes, powerfully setting men and women free from the prison of a fallen nature. No wonder the Bible boasts that this new arrangement is "a better covenant...established on better promises" (Heb. 8:6).

Declare Who You Are in Christ

I declare that I am a child of the covenant! God has committed Himself to me and has promised never to leave me or forsake me. I respond by making a similar worshipful commitment to Him. By the grace and help of God, I choose to never leave Him nor forsake Him. Because of our covenant, my battles and my burdens now belong to God, and I believe He will intervene for me miraculously. In like manner, God's battles and God's burdens now belong to me. He will fight to ensure that I emerge more than a conqueror in all the trials of life. Therefore, out of love for Him, I assume the responsibility of fighting the good fight of faith and doing all I can do to advance His kingdom in this world. In Jesus's name, amen!

Additional reading: Psalm 25:14; Matthew 26:26–29; 2 Corinthians 3:5–11; Hebrews 9:13–15; 13:20–21

Chapter 33

GOOD SOLDIERS
OF JESUS CHRIST

*You therefore must endure hardship as
a good soldier of Jesus Christ.*
—2 TIMOTHY 2:3, NKJV

A GOOD SOLDIER is known by seven primary traits: obedience, discipline, endurance, tenacity, fearlessness, bravery, and willingness to sacrifice all. Countless thousands have developed such admirable qualities for causes that are earthly and temporal. But our cause is heavenly, eternal, and far more important. How much more should we be spiritually militant individuals of soldier-like courage and commitment, unflinching in the heat of battle!

One of our biggest challenges is the dual nature of the war in which we are engaged, for it rages on two primary battlefronts: one external and the other internal.

The *external war* is being waged against a very real, yet unseen enemy—"spiritual forces of evil in the heavenly places" (Eph. 6:12). Satan and his demonic underlings have struggled for many centuries to achieve their goal of global dominance, and they have succeeded in deceiving "the whole world" (Rev. 12:9). Threatened by any proclamation of truth, they constantly "make war" against those "who keep the commandments of God and have the testimony of Jesus Christ" (Rev. 12:17). These evil powers greatly influence the world around us, which in turn pits itself against all who embrace biblical principles, so that the church is often at odds with the culture. Yet our battle is not against "flesh and blood" (Eph. 6:12) but against "the prince of the power of the air, the spirit who now works in the sons of disobedience" (Eph. 2:2).

The *internal war* is against the fallen nature of the flesh. James, the brother of Jesus, shined a spotlight on this enemy when he posed the question, "From where do wars and fightings among you come? Is it not…from your lusts which war in your members?" (James 4:1, MKJV). Paul also confessed, "For I delight in the law of God according to the inner man, but I see another law in my members, warring against the law of my mind and bringing me into captivity to the law of sin which is in my members" (Rom. 7:22–23). Prior to salvation this enemy is overwhelming, and though some unsaved people do succeed in living disciplined lives, on an ultimate level this foe is unbeatable without God's help.

Both the external war and the internal war gather to one primary, central battlefield in a child of God—our minds. Yet the captain of our salvation has given us an awesome promise:

> For the weapons of our warfare are not carnal, but mighty through God to the pulling down of strongholds, casting down imaginations and every high thing that exalts itself against the knowledge of God, bringing every thought into captivity to the obedience of Christ.
> —2 Corinthians 10:4–5

WHAT IS A STRONGHOLD?

A stronghold is an area of influence where the enemy resides in order to maintain control over an individual, over regions, or society as a whole. When we allow wrong, evil, dark, or negative thought patterns to dominate our minds, a stronghold is reared. Sometimes these are self-created, sometimes they are the result of societal trends, sometimes they result from damaging human relationships, or sometimes they are of demonic origin. Regardless of the source the church has been given sufficient weaponry to win. Some of the weapons of warfare in our arsenal include:

+ **The Word of God**: When Jesus faced off with the devil in the wilderness, though He was the Word made flesh, He resorted to quoting the written Word in order to conquer. Three times He responded to Satan with the statement, "It is written," then quoted a scripture suitable in overcoming the temptation (Matt. 4:1–11). Satan is not omnipresent, and each individual Christian does not experience a personal confrontation with him daily. (In fact, believers who are constantly talking to the devil are really deceiving themselves.) The prince of darkness can only be at one place, at one time—so it would be impossible for him to personally attack over two billion believers in the world daily. Of course, he has an army of demons under his authority that do attack us often. We should respond to them just as Jesus did.

+ **The blood of Jesus:** Nothing in the enemy's arsenal can match the blood of Jesus in authority and power. The cross is where Jesus triumphed over satanic "principalities and powers" so our victory is an established fact (Col. 2:15, NKJV). Confessing His shed blood is an instantaneous thrust of irresistible authority. Many believers are taught to claim the blood of Jesus during spiritual warfare; however, some make an erroneous assumption in practicing this method. They "claim the blood" as if they are requesting something external to pour over them temporarily. Instead, it should be a confession of an ever-present, internal condition. Jesus revealed that true believers "drink" His blood (John 6:53–55). Whatever we drink is inseparably a part of us. Therefore, as our natural blood flows constantly through our circulatory system (whether we confess it or not) so the spiritual blood of Jesus flows constantly through our spirits, rejuvenating our righteousness and strength with every passing moment (whether we confess it or not). No wonder no weapon formed against us can prosper.

+ **The name of Jesus:** One of the most powerful passages dealing with this weapon is Luke 10:17–20. The seventy disciples had just returned to Jesus testifying, "Lord, even the demons are subject to us through Your name." To this He responded, "I saw Satan as lightning fall from heaven." If the name of the Lord was that powerful even though the disciples had not yet been born again, how much more powerful it is in toppling the enemy's strongholds once believers have been regenerated by God's power.

In considering just these three weapons, no wonder, in advance, John declared concerning the attack of Satan on the church in the last days:

> They overcame him by the blood of the Lamb and by the word of their testimony, and they loved not their lives unto the death.
>
> —REVELATION 12:11

So rise up "good soldier of Jesus Christ" (2 Tim. 2:3) and "fight the good fight of faith" (1 Tim. 6:12). We can only properly utilize our weapons and overcome in this spiritual war if we tenaciously believe in the promises of God, the faithfulness of God, and the calling we have received from God. And by the way, you need to remember, if you are truly saved:

> The battle belongs to the LORD.
>
> —1 SAMUEL 17:47

DECLARE WHO YOU ARE IN CHRIST

I declare that I am a good soldier of Jesus Christ! I make a commitment to live a life of obedience, discipline, endurance, tenacity, fearlessness, bravery, and sacrifice. Because I am in covenant with God, my battles are His battles, but it is also true that His battles are my battles. Therefore, it is my responsibility to fight the good fight of faith, not only for my own spiritual survival, but also so that the kingdom of God might advance in this world. In order to stand against the schemes of the devil, I put on the whole armor of God: the helmet of salvation, the breastplate of righteousness, the belt of truth, and the shoes of the gospel. In every situation I wield the two-edged sword of the Spirit, which is the Word of God. I declare that I will prevail by the blood of the Lamb and the word of my testimony. I accept my calling to be a champion for the truth. In Jesus's name, amen!

Additional reading: Exodus 15:1–3; Ephesians 6:11–18; 2 Timothy 2:1–4; Revelation 19:11–14

Chapter 34

THE HOUSEHOLD OF FAITH

*Therefore, as we have opportunity, let us do good to all
people, especially to those who are of the household of faith.*
—GALATIANS 6:10

T HERE ARE TWO primary definitions assigned to the word
faith. First, our faith can be the sum of religious principles on
which we base our lives; second, it can be the act of believing in God
and trusting His promises.

The word *household* can mean either a family or all those residing
in the same home. As born-again believers we are part of the same
family, dwelling under the same roof of the redemptive love of God.
Our privilege is to experience life together with hearts intertwined
in covenant relationship. The glue that holds us together is not some
denominational affiliation, but our mutual faith in our Savior, the
Lord Jesus Christ.

Strangely the word *faith* appears only twice in the Old Testament,
but over 240 times in the New Testament—so it is definitely an
emphasis in this era. There is much to be learned about this spiritual
"substance" Paul described as a "mystery" (Heb. 11:1; 1 Tim. 3:9).

The following ten insights are some of the most important:

+ **Faith is a gift from God.** Ephesians 2:8 declares, "By
grace you have been saved through faith, and this is not
of yourselves. It is the gift of God." A gift is not something earned; it is given freely as an expression of love. God
so loved us that He gave us the capacity to believe. The
Scriptures title Jesus "the author and finisher of our faith"
(Heb. 12:2). He initiates faith within our hearts and then
continues growing and developing that faith within us for
the remainder of our lives.

- **Faith is allocated by God.** Every child of God is granted a "measure of faith" (Rom. 12:3). In other words, in His omniscience God anticipates all that His offspring will be called to do in the kingdom, and all the battles and challenges they will face in life. In advance He assigns enough faith to each one of us that we might succeed in every arena. Because of this, it is "not of works, so that no one should boast" (Eph. 2:9).

- **Faith is awakened by the Word of God.** "Faith comes by hearing, and hearing by the Word of God" (Rom. 10:17). The written Word (the *logos*) stirs faith in those who hear it with receptive hearts. The living Word (the *rhema*—God speaking to us personally) causes this awakening to an even greater degree.

- **Faith empowers us to receive the Spirit of God.** We "receive the promise of the Spirit through faith" (Gal. 3:14). Then, after we are begotten of the Word and born of the Spirit, we move through life speaking "the word of faith," aided by the "Spirit of faith" (a title for the Holy Spirit), thus empowered to accomplish great things for the kingdom of God (2 Cor. 4:13).

- **Faith makes us righteous in the sight of God.** Christians are "justified by faith" (Rom. 5:1). To be justified means to be legally acquitted of all guilt, as if we never sinned, and recognized as righteous in the sight of God. Contrary to all other religions, the miracle of Christianity is that "with the heart, one believes unto righteousness" (Rom. 10:10).

- **Faith is a spiritual weapon.** Paul exhorted Timothy to "fight the good fight of faith" and to "lay hold on eternal life" (1 Tim. 6:12). There are so many adversaries on this journey from time to eternity, within and without. We war against literal powers of darkness, as well as dark attitudes and thoughts that churn within our own hearts. As spiritual soldiers we are encouraged to wear the "breastplate of faith" and take "the shield of faith" in order to "extinguish all the fiery arrows of the evil one" (1 Thess. 5:8; Eph. 6:16).

+ **Faith grants ultimate victory.** First John 5:4 says that "whoever is born of God overcomes the world, and the victory that overcomes the world is our faith." There is nothing that this world will throw at us that faith cannot overpower, even the worst thing—death. If faith can overcome the most grievous adversary, it can certainly empower us to rise above lesser problems. No wonder the Scripture uses the past tense in declaring that "you have overcome the evil one" (1 John 2:14). It is as good as done.

+ **Faith activates resurrection power.** At the grave site of Lazarus, Jesus asserted, "I am the resurrection and the life. He who believes in Me, though he may die, yet shall he live" (John 11:25). When we believe that the Father raised the Son of God from the dead, our souls are saved (Rom. 10:8–10), but then we go on to believe God will raise us from the grave also to live forever in His presence.

+ **Faith will bring us to perfection eternally.** Ephesians 4:11–13 reveals that the fivefold ministry (pastors, evangelists, teachers, apostles, and prophets) exists to build up the body of Christ "until we all come into the unity of the faith and of the knowledge of the Son of God, into a complete man, to the measure of the stature of the fullness of Christ." The New King James says "to a perfect man." So it is faith that will bring the entire body of Christ to perfection, completion, and fullness and cause us to finally emerge in the full image of the firstborn Son.

+ **Faith without works is dead.** James declared that "faith without works is dead," or nonexistent (James 2:26). Works will automatically result from real faith, and they indicate its existence. As General Booth, founder of the Salvation Army, explained, "Faith and works should travel side by side, step answering to step, like the legs of men walking. First faith, and then works; and then faith again, and then works again—until they can scarcely distinguish which is the one and which is the other."[1]

DECLARE WHO YOU ARE IN CHRIST

I declare that I am a member of the household of faith! Knowing that faith pleases God, I have determined to respond to the challenges of life with unwavering trust in God's Word. Because I believe in the name of the Lord, His crucifixion and resurrection, I already have overcome the world. I refuse to stagger at the promise of God through unbelief, so that my faith might result in "praise, glory, and honor at the revelation of Jesus Christ" (1 Pet. 1:7)—when the author and the finisher of my faith returns in all His glory. In Jesus's name, amen!

Additional reading: Matthew 17:20; Mark 11:22–24; Luke 22:31–32; Hebrews 10:23; 11:6; 1 Peter 1:6–9

Chapter 35

ORACLES OF GOD

If anyone speaks, let him speak as the oracles of God.
—1 Peter 4:11

THE WORD ORACLE means a divinely inspired communication. It can also refer to the person used as God's mouthpiece. The prophetic utterance is an oracle, and the one who speaks the prophetic utterance is an oracle, as the passage above implies.

This term is found three other times in the New Testament and is always a reference to the Word of God, translated from the Greek word *logion* (pronounced log'-ee-on):

+ In Acts 7:38 Stephen, the first martyr of the church, preached how Moses received the "living oracles to give to us"—the revelations he received from God on Mount Sinai.

+ In Romans 3:2 Paul explained the advantage of being Jewish, claiming, "the oracles of God were entrusted to them," referring to all Old Testament Scripture.

+ In Hebrews 5:12 the author states that the people reading that epistle should already be teachers, but they needed someone to teach them again "the first principles of the oracles of God," the basic doctrines of both the old and new covenants.

Only in 1 Peter 4:11 do we find the word *oracle* given as a name for believers, challenging them to measure up to this high calling. The most remarkable aspect is that Peter said, "If *anyone* speaks," so this is not just a potential residing in apostles, prophets, pastors, evangelists, or teachers. Any sincere Christian can be used of God this way.

The Tree of Life Version of Scripture translates this passage, "Whoever speaks, let it be as one speaking the utterances of God." And the New Living Translation exhorts believers to "speak as though God himself were speaking." It is one thing to echo what God has already said (declaring the written Word, or the *logos*); it's another thing to be the vehicle through which He speaks (declaring the living Word, or the *rhema*). But both are legitimate ways of fulfilling this calling.

Actually there are four levels of speaking as an oracle:

+ **Speaking positive, godly words:** Believers should first purge out of their speech all words of fear, doubt, bitterness, resentment, discouragement, or selfishness—the kind of negative words that God would never speak—and instead, speak words of faith, confidence, love, forgiveness, courage, justice, and generosity because what you say is what you get. Proverbs 18:21 says, "Death and life are in the power of the tongue, and those who love it will eat its fruit." The word translated "power" is the Hebrew *yad* (pronounced *yawd*), and it means an open hand. So every confession that goes out of your mouth is like an open hand reaching up to receive what has just been said. Be careful what you say. Speak positive, faith-filled words in harmony with Scripture.

+ **Speaking biblical truth:** A true believer should be constantly confessing and declaring the written Word of God, "speaking the truth in love" (Eph. 4:15)—functioning as a "letter of Christ" (a communication from the Messiah) in all their day-to-day encounters (2 Cor. 3:3).

+ **Speaking prophetically:** The third level relates to far more than just maintaining positive, godly attitudes or quoting the Bible. It means sharing truth with others under the inspiration of the Holy Spirit "that it may minister grace unto the hearers" (Eph. 4:29, KJV). At times it may involve receiving and declaring "the word of knowledge" or "the word of wisdom": flashes of inspired insight concerning situations in people's lives and God's divine directives concerning how they should act or react (1 Cor. 12:8).

+ **Speaking with divine authority:** Finally, when believers not only *speak* but also *pray* as oracles of God, they tend to imitate the firstborn Son of God. Jesus did not plead with the Father to heal the sick or deliver the oppressed. Knowing that He was God's mouthpiece, He commanded them to be healed and set free. He taught His followers to use a similar method, as in the following often-quoted passages:

"For it is not you who speak, but the Spirit of your Father who speaks through you" (Matt. 10:20).

"If you have faith as a grain of mustard seed, you will say to this mountain, 'Move from here to there,' and it will move. And nothing will be impossible for you" (Matt. 17:20).

"If you had faith as a grain of mustard seed, you could say to this mulberry tree, 'Be uprooted and planted in the sea,' and it would obey you" (Luke 17:6).

Certainly there are many qualifying factors that determine what we can say, how we can say it, and when it will be effective. We cannot indiscriminately decree whatever we want whenever we want and without fail watch it come to pass. To think so would be absurd. However, these passages do reveal that Christians have an authority, an ability to speak as God's representatives, which is really astounding. He did say, "Whatever you bind on earth will be bound in heaven, and whatever you loose on earth will be loosed in heaven" (Matt. 18:18).[1]

The key is yieldedness, as Jesus indicated in the following passage: "If you abide in Me, and My words abide in you, you will ask what you desire, and it shall be done for you" (John 15:7, NKJV).

Functioning on this level of oneness with the Lord would cause His desire to become your desire and your desire to blend in with His desire—so you are not speaking independent of His will or His Word. Jeremiah brought balance to this whole concept when he said, "Who is he who speaks and it comes to pass, unless the Lord has commanded it?" (Lam. 3:37).

So we have to be sensitive, inspired, alert, obedient, and bold. Jesus was the firstborn oracle of a family of oracles. He taught us how to do it, saying, "The words that I say to you I do not speak on

My own authority. But the Father who lives in Me does the works" (John 14:10).

Now He challenges us to walk in His footsteps.

DECLARE WHO YOU ARE IN CHRIST

I declare that I am called to speak as an oracle of God! I consecrate my heart and my mouth to God and intend to purge out of my speech words of fear, unbelief, unforgiveness, weakness, and hatred. Instead I choose to speak words of courage, faith, forgiveness, strength, and compassion. I reject the negative and cling to the positive. I am determined to speak the truth of God's Word in love to a world desperately in need of hearing from heaven. I pray the Holy Spirit will awaken in me the word of wisdom and the word of knowledge that I might be God's mouthpiece, prophetically sharing His wisdom with others. In Jesus's name, amen!

Additional reading: Joshua 1:8; 1 Samuel 3:19; Psalm 36:1; Matthew 10:19–20

Chapter 36

A ROYAL PRIESTHOOD

But you are a chosen generation, *a royal priesthood*,
a holy nation, His own special people.
—1 PETER 2:9, NKJV

J ESUS WAS BOTH King and Priest.

As the "KING OF KINGS," He manifested divine dominion in this world: reigning over sin, sickness, Satan, evil spirits, temptations, negative circumstances, and His own flesh (Rev. 19:16). He ruled over hate with love, depression with joy, and judgmental attitudes with the mercy of God. Irresistible in sovereign power, He even conquered the greatest archenemies of the human race: sin, Satan, death, hell, and the grave.

As the "great High Priest," Jesus lived a life of service, serving the Father with adoration and serving the human race with compassion (Heb. 4:14). In priestly intercession He stood in the gap for the needy, providing atonement for their sins and reconciling their wayward hearts to God.

In both of these areas the firstborn Son of God became a living example of how we are to walk in this world, as spiritual kings and priests, or as 1 Peter 2:9 puts it, "a royal priesthood." All children of God bear this dual image. Revelation 1:6 discloses that Jesus already "made us kings and priests to His God and Father," so this is not just a futuristic calling.

As kings we wield God-given authority over the sin nature and over a demonically infested and broken world system filled with fear, anxiety, perversity, and unbelief. We reign by manifesting the nature of the kingdom of God—traits such as courage, peace, purity, and faith.

As priests we minister to God in worship and serve the needs of others. Our greatest privilege as priests is to reconcile fallen human beings to a right relationship with God. (See 2 Corinthians 5:18–19.)

Old Testament priests did that by officiating over the sacrifice of animals to provide a temporary atonement for sin. We do it by leading people to the cross where the blood of Jesus blots out their sins forever.

At the onset of Israel's wilderness journey God revealed that this dual calling was His original will for all the seed of Abraham, even under the old covenant. He told Moses to communicate to the people:

> Now therefore, if you will faithfully obey My voice and keep My covenant, then you shall be My special possession out of all the nations, for all the earth is Mine. And you will be to Me *a kingdom of priests* and a holy nation.
> —Exodus 19:5–6

Yes, God wanted every Israelite to be a part of His kingdom—both male and female, old and young—to reign in life victoriously and to have priestly access into His presence. That intention was never fully realized, however, because the Israelites as a nation rejected priesthood intimacy with God two distinct times.

When the fire of God descended on Mount Sinai and the thunderclap of His voice gave the Ten Commandments, the Israelites cried aloud to Moses, "You speak to us, and we will listen. But do not let God speak to us, lest we die" (Exod. 20:19). In other words, they were saying, "We don't want this kind of intimate contact with God. It is too fearful, too overwhelming. We don't want this priestly access."

About forty days later they made a false idol, a golden calf, and exalted it as their god. On that pivotal and disappointing day it appears they forfeited the priesthood through their idolatry because that calling passed to the tribe of Levi (for they alone stood with Moses against the worship of the idol). After that it became necessary for ordinary Israelites to come to the Levitical priests in order to reach God.

Of course, all of that changed when Jesus's death, burial, and resurrection shifted the covenants. Now God's original dream has been reinstated in even greater depth. We no longer require priestly mediators, because every child of God belongs to a "holy priesthood"

(1 Pet. 2:5), and every born-again believer enjoys "access by one Spirit to the Father" (Eph. 2:18).

Our hearts should be filled with awe even now at the profoundness of such a great blessing. But surely when this earthly pilgrimage is over, we will realize all the more the goodness of God toward us when we join the heavenly multitude singing a new song to the Lamb of God:

> You are worthy....For You were slain, and have redeemed us to God by Your blood out of every tribe and tongue and people and nation, and have made us *kings and priests* unto our God; and we shall reign on the earth.
>
> —REVELATION 5:9–10

Until that glorious day comes, let us walk in our spiritual identity by the perfect blend of reigning and serving—and all for the glory of the Lord.

DECLARE WHO YOU ARE IN CHRIST

I declare that I am a part of a royal priesthood! I have been empowered by God's Word and by God's Spirit to reign as a spiritual king over every negative thing I face in life. I have also been empowered as a spiritual priest to minister to God in worship and to live a life of godly service to others. Reigning and serving are very much a part of who I am in Christ. My elder brother is the King of kings and the great High Priest. He is the firstborn Son of God who established the king/priest calling for all other sons and daughters of God to follow. I accept this challenge and rejoice in this privilege. In Jesus's name, amen!

Additional reading: Exodus 30:30; Isaiah 61:1–6; Joel 2:17; Revelation 20:1–6

Chapter 37

WITNESSES

But you shall receive power when the Holy Spirit comes
upon you. And you shall be My *witnesses* in Jerusalem, and
in all Judea and Samaria, and to the ends of the earth.
—ACTS 1:8

Awitness is someone who publicly affirms by word or
action a certain belief or conviction, has personal knowledge,
or offers evidence or proof.

Because we have *personal knowledge* of the Lord Jesus Christ, it
is our responsibility to *publicly affirm* that He truly is the Savior of
the world. Our transformed lives should be sufficient *evidence* that
He rose from the dead, ascended to heaven, and is presently Lord
over all nations.

The Greek word translated "witnesses" is *martus* (prounouced
mar'-toos) also translated "martyr" in Scripture. So a real witness
biblically is someone willing to die (literally) for the cause of Christ
or die (spiritually speaking) to all the allurements and deceptions of
this world.

THE FIRST WITNESS

The first mention chronologically of the word *witness* in Scripture
is actually a reference to something God did. In response to Abel's
sacrifice He provided a supernatural sign:

> By faith Abel offered to God a more excellent sacrifice than
> Cain, through which he *obtained witness* that he was righteous,
> God testifying of his gifts; and through it he being dead still
> speaks.
> **—HEBREWS 11:4, NKJV**

We are not told exactly what the "witness" was, but based on a
later pattern, it was probably visible, supernatural fire sent from

heaven to consume Abel's sacrificial lamb. Why would God do that? To reveal that Cain's sacrifice of the fruit of the ground (representing man's works) was insufficient and that a blood sacrifice was necessary for sins to be forgiven, for worship to be accepted, and for a relationship with God to be restored.

THE BEGINNING YEARS

In the beginning centuries, prior to the law, the primary way God "witnessed" truth to the human race was through the conscience:

> For when Gentiles, who do not have the law, do by nature the things contained in the law, these, not having the law, are a law unto themselves, who show the work of the law written in their hearts, *their conscience also bearing witness*, while their conflicting thoughts accuse or even excuse them, in the day when, according to my gospel, God will judge the secrets of men through Jesus Christ.
>
> —ROMANS 2:14–16

The conscience is that inward sense of what is morally right and morally wrong. In sensitive and decent people it is brimming with the desire to do what is right. It is so translated from the Greek word *suneidésis* (pronounced soon-i'-day-sis), which means co-perception.[1] So being sensitive to your conscience basically means seeing things as God sees them.

Unfortunately the conscience is defiled and undependable until true salvation takes place. When that happens, God promises to "cleanse your conscience from dead works to serve the living God" (Heb. 9:14). You are then called to hold "the mystery of the faith in a pure conscience," like someone raising a blazing torch in a very dark place (1 Tim. 3:9).

THE TABERNACLE OF WITNESS

The next milestone came when God gave Moses the design for something He called "the tabernacle of witness" (Num. 17:7, NKJV). The MEV says "tent of witness." This sacred tent had three chambers (outer court, holy place, and holy of holies). For many years it was the only place in the entire world where God met with people. In it were six pieces of furniture: the altar of sacrifice, the laver, the table of showbread, the altar of incense, the menorah lampstand, and the ark of the covenant.

The tabernacle "witnessed" five vitally important things to the Israelite people (and to all of us):

+ God desires to dwell among His people and have a relationship with them.

+ A mediator is required to successfully reach God (the priests in that era).

+ A blood sacrifice is required for sinful human beings to be reconciled to God.

+ God is holy and those desiring to commune with Him must be holy.

+ God would rather show mercy than judgment (the mercy seat in the holy of holies was God's representative throne on the earth).

All of these things prophetically "witnessed" of the new covenant to come when the perfect sacrifice would be offered by the great High Priest, the only true mediator between God and men, the Lord Jesus Christ.

PENTECOST POWER

We need to ponder the real reason God gave the baptism of the Holy Spirit ("the promise of the Father") on the Day of Pentecost (Acts 1:4). It was not just to bless and edify believers, but rather to enable them to more effectively witness the truth. They were "endued with power"—Greek *dunamis*, also translated "mighty" and "miracle"[2]—not just for their own spiritual advancement, but also for the sake of others (Luke 24:49, NKJV). Though the apostles were considered "illiterate and uneducated men" (Acts 4:13), this empowerment equipped them to shake Jerusalem with revival:

> God also *bore them witness* with signs and wonders and diverse miracles and with gifts of the Holy Spirit distributed according to His own will.
> —HEBREWS 2:4

The rushing mighty wind and the consuming fire from heaven that visited the Upper Room has since blown and burned to every continent and every nation. The world has never been the same. God's passion hasn't changed, for the ancient prophecy hovers over us still:

> And this gospel of the kingdom will be preached in all the world *as a witness* to all the nations, and then the end will come.
>
> —MATTHEW 24:14, NKJV

The Creator is still working on the reacquisition of this planet, and He is depending on us to help Him accomplish this feat. In a world full of many false deities, His voice echoes:

> You are My *witnesses*, says the LORD, that I am God.
>
> —ISAIAH 43:12

How can we give sleep to our eyes or slumber to our eyelids until we accomplish this holy task, until every man and woman has heard of the salvation that can be found in Jesus alone?

It's time to die to self and come alive to this purpose—above all other things!

DECLARE WHO YOU ARE IN CHRIST

I declare that I am a witness of the Lord Jesus Christ! My changed life is sufficient proof, not only that Jesus rose from the dead, but also that He resurrects people from the death-dealing curse that has devoured this planet. I declare that by the grace of God I will have an impact on my sphere of influence. I will be a "true witness" who "delivers souls" (Prov. 14:25). I believe that God will work with me by imparting "signs and wonders and diverse miracles and with gifts of the Holy Spirit" (Heb. 2:4). Yes, if I witness for the King, the King will witness for me. In Jesus's name, amen!

Additional reading: Isaiah 44:8; John 15:27; Acts 2:32; 3:15; 5:30–32; Hebrews 12:1; Revelation 11:3–13

PART 6

YOU ARE VICTORIOUS

Chapter 38

THE HEAD

And the LORD will make you *the head* and not the tail;
you will only be above and you will not be beneath, if you
listen to the commandments of the LORD your God, which
I am commanding you today, to observe and to do them.
—**DEUTERONOMY 28:13**

THIS DECLARATION OF headship was the high point of a very notable day. God wanted the choice between "life and death, blessing and curse" to be rehearsed in the minds of the Israelites at the very beginning of their entrance into the Promised Land (Deut. 30:19).

Six tribes stood on the slopes of Mount Gerizim shouting "Amen" to the blessings of the law. About five hundred yards away the other six tribes stood on the slopes of Mount Ebal shouting "Amen" to the curses. (See Deuteronomy 27:12–13.) A special altar was erected in the valley between the mountains and from that area the Levites declared the word of the Lord, including the proclamation of headship, which is our key verse. (To read all the blessings and curses, see Deuteronomy 27:12–28:68.)

GOD'S MOTIVE

Of all the nations of the world, why did God choose Israel for such a high calling? Deuteronomy 7:7–8 explains:

> The LORD did not set His love on you nor choose you because you were more in number than any of the peoples, for you were *the fewest of all the peoples*. But it is because the LORD loved you and because He kept the oath which He swore to your fathers.

So God's main motives were His great love for the children of Israel and faithfulness to the promise He made to Abraham, Isaac, and Jacob. Ironically it seems also to be more than just a coincidence that Israel was the least likely nation to succeed on its own. This could be called "The Mustard Seed Principle"—a major personality trait of the kingdom of God, as well as the God of that kingdom.

Just as the mustard seed is the "least of all seeds," but becomes "the greatest among herbs," so the Creator loves to choose people and things that are considered the lowest, the last, and the least and then transform them into the highest, the first, and the greatest—to reveal His power and to give glory to His name (Matt. 13:31–32; see also Romans 9:17). Knowing this inclination of God should build confidence in believers who feel overlooked, ostracized, unqualified, or incapable.

God's Intention

God intended Israel to be the "head" in every arena of human experience: politically, militarily, socially, scientifically, educationally, monetarily, materially, religiously, and spiritually. In achieving excellence and preeminence, they were to become the exemplary nation—in a sense, God's "firstborn"—a living testimony of what can happen when an entire nation walks in covenant with God (Exod. 4:22).

What happened to hinder the plan? For a season it was astoundingly successful, but then everything fell apart and totally the opposite happened. The Israelites ended up becoming slaves to five successive Gentile empires—the Assyrians, the Babylonians, the Persians, the Grecians, and finally the Romans.[1] So for centuries instead of being "the head," they actually became "the tail," just as God forewarned (Deut. 28:43–44). A single, two-letter word was the primary stumbling block—the fifth word in the following verse:

> Now it will be, if you diligently obey the voice of the LORD your God, being careful to do all His commandments which I am commanding you today, then the LORD your God will set you high above all the nations of the earth.
>
> —DEUTERONOMY 28:1

The word *if* was the culprit. God would exalt them only *if* they obeyed. God would help them only *if* they were submissive. So under the old covenant especially, headship depended primarily on human performance, the ability of the Israelite people to flawlessly abide by the law. The Israelites on Mount Ebal must have trembled as they heard one of the final proclamations:

> Cursed is he who does not confirm all the words of this law by doing them.
>
> —DEUTERONOMY 27:26

From that moment they shouted "Amen," the heavy demand of impeccably keeping the 613 commandments of the Torah loomed over them as an ominous, dark cloud. As rebellion increased, over a period of centuries, their situation grew increasingly hopeless. It looked like the covenant was going to collapse in utter failure.

But then the Messiah came, the One the Prophet Micah called "the breaker," or in other words, the One who brings the breakthrough (Mic. 2:13, KJV).

THE MYSTERIOUS TURNING POINT

The breakthrough miracle providing headship took place when the Messiah walked among men. But Jesus was much more than just a man; He was "God manifested in the flesh" (1 Tim. 3:16, NKJV). After thirty-three years He was crucified and sunk to the lowest possible place of degradation; the One who was absolutely pure "bore our sins in His own body on the tree" (1 Pet. 2:24). He absorbed all the vileness of the human race—past, present, and future—so that He became the vilest of all. He who was rightfully "the head" instead became "the tail" by offering Himself as our substitute.

But not for long. Three days later the "Spirit of holiness" quickened Him back to life, and He rose again (Rom. 1:4). That pivotal event caused more than just an earthquake; it triggered a "heavenquake" with rumblings that went all the way back to the fall of Adam. God's mighty power was released:

> Which He worked in Christ when He raised Him from the dead and seated Him at His right hand in the heavenly places, far above all principality and power and might and dominion, and every name that is named, not only in this age but also in that which is to come. And He put all things under His feet,

and gave Him to be head over all things to the church, which is
His body, the fullness of Him who fills all in all.

—Ephesians 1:19–23, nkjv

The Amplified Bible, Classic Edition, insightfully adds this is *"a
headship exercised throughout the church."*

So Jesus came down to our level in order to lift us up to His
level—that the sin-stained seed of Adam could experience headship
as well. (See Ephesians 2:5–6; Isaiah 57:15.) Through the blood that
cleanses us, the Spirit that enlivens us, the name that sanctifies us,
and the covenant that empowers us, we are exalted over every enemy
of the human race: sin, satanic powers, self, the grave, death, and
eternal destruction.

Because Jesus is the head and we are His body, if all things are
under His feet, all things are now under our feet as well. Since His
enemies have been made His "footstool," our enemies have been
made our footstool too (Ps. 110:1; see also Matthew 22:44). Once
we repent, our personal failures become stepping-stones instead of
stumbling stones. Instead of being executioners leading us to the
gallows, they become lessons in life leading us to a place of wisdom.
Instead of groveling helplessly under their domination, we subject
them to the power of faith and master them in the name of the Lord.
In other words, we achieve and manifest headship.

One day this amazing calling will be perfected in us, when we
"shine forth as the sun" in the kingdom of our Father (Matt. 13:43).
Believers will then rule and reign as kings and priests over a restored
paradise world and the new creation to come. On a universal level
we will be the head and not the tail—the highest of all created
beings, sons of God, the ruling hierarchy of a kingdom that will
never be moved.

Declare Who You Are in Christ

*I declare that I am the head, and not the tail; I live above
always, and I am never beneath! Even in my trials, tribu-
lations, and personal battles I am triumphant, for nothing
can separate me from the love of God. No weapon formed
against me shall prosper. All things work together for my*

*good. I am either up, or I am getting up. If all things are
under Jesus's feet, all things are under my feet: sin, sickness,
Satan, and even my own past failures. Because Jesus has
ascended far above all things, I have ascended far above
all things. I am seated with Him in heavenly places. I am
enthroned with the Lord Jesus Christ and reigning with
Him even now. In Jesus's name, amen!*

Additional reading: Psalm 27:6; Micah 2:13; Matthew 21:42 (KJV);
Romans 16:20; Ephesians 4:15; Colossians 2:10, 18–19

Chapter 39

HEIRS OF GOD

*The Spirit Himself bears witness with our spirits that we
are the children of God, and if children, then heirs: heirs
of God and joint-heirs with Christ, if indeed we suffer
with Him, that we may also be glorified with Him.*
—ROMANS 8:16–17

A N HEIR IS one who is entitled by law to receive the estate of
another; the heir is the rightful recipient of certain properties, possessions, endowments, positions of influence, or qualities of
character passed on from a parent or predecessor.

In Hebrews 9:16–17 Jesus is described as a "testator" (one who
draws up a will or testament to be enforced at his death). The New
Testament (made up of twenty-seven books) is the will that reveals
what the crucified and resurrected Lord left to His heirs.

There are a number of names for God's people in this portion
of the Word that refer to the children of God as heirs. Each one
reveals a unique aspect of our inheritance, such as:

+ Heirs of salvation (Heb. 1:14, KJV)

+ Heirs of promise (Heb. 6:17)

+ Heirs of the righteousness that comes by faith (Heb. 11:7)

+ Heirs of the world (Rom. 4:13)

+ Heirs of the kingdom (James 2:5)

+ Heirs of the grace of life (1 Pet. 3:7)

+ Heirs according to the hope of eternal life (Titus 3:7)

Just reading this list should leave us in a state of breathless awe.
These names for God's people describe a corporate inheritance
shared among the entire body of Christ—astounding benefits that
God has transferred to all His "beneficiaries."[1]

GLIMPSING THE PROFOUNDNESS

If we are heirs of God, what is the most comprehensive, yet simple way of describing the fullness of what we have inherited? The answer is simply profound:

+ We have inherited *all that God is.*
+ We have inherited *all that God has.*

We have inherited His Word, His glory, His perfection, His love, and much more. In His great intercessory prayer over the church Jesus declared this grand transfer in advance (in a sense, He was reading the will):

> Father...I have given them the words which You gave Me....I have given them the glory which You gave me, that they may be one even as We are one: I in them and You in Me, that they may be perfect in unity....I have declared Your name to them, and will declare it, that the love with which You have loved Me may be in them, and I in them.
> —JOHN 17:1, 8, 22–23, 26

According to this powerful passage, Jesus even passed to us the inheritance of the oneness with the Father He enjoyed. How amazing is that! His peace and His joy also belong to us (John 14:27; 15:11), as well as His wisdom (1 Cor. 1:30), His knowledge (Isa. 53:11), and His authority (Luke 10:19). And the list goes on.

According to our beginning verse we are also referred to as "joint-heirs with Christ," which means equal heirs. So one good way of determining our inheritance is to look at the inheritance of the first-born Son of God, for His spiritual condition and His destiny reveal the grand legacy that has been passed down to every child of God.

Colossians says concerning Jesus, "It pleased the Father that in Him all fullness should dwell" and "in Him dwells all the fullness of the Godhead bodily" (Col. 1:19; 2:9, MKJV). Then John 1:16 makes the astounding statement, "Of His fullness we have all received" (NKJV).

Hebrews 1:2 declares that God has "in these last days spoken to us by His Son, whom He has appointed heir of all things, and through whom He made the world." Then Revelation 21:7 gives the incredible promise, "He who overcomes shall inherit all things, and I will be his God, and he shall be My son."

The full depth of how this divine generosity will manifest in us is a mystery only God fully comprehends, but whatever it entails, it will surely be absolutely spectacular.

Our Inheritance Is "in Him"

If we have made Jesus the Lord of our lives, then we are under His headship and a part of His body. This places us "in Christ" ("in the Messiah") where all that He is passes down to us as a spiritual impartation.

Ephesians 1:11 declares that "*in Him* also we have received an inheritance."

These two words—"in Him"—indicate our position of inheritance. Therefore, it is vital to search out every scripture in the New Testament containing the words "in Him," "in whom" (in reference to Jesus), or "in Christ" to discover the spiritual deposit that has been placed there for us. For instance, we have inherited:

+ **Access into the Father's presence:** "In whom we have boldness and access with confidence through faith in Him" (Eph. 3:12, NKJV).

+ **Jesus's resurrection life:** "For the law of the Spirit of life in Christ Jesus has set me free from the law of sin and death" (Rom. 8:2).

+ **A new creation status:** "Therefore, if anyone is in Christ, he is a new creation; old things have passed away; behold, all things have become new" (2 Cor. 5:17, NKJV).

+ **Jesus's righteousness:** "God made Him who knew no sin to be sin for us, that we might become the righteousness of God in Him" (2 Cor. 5:21).

+ **Every spiritual blessing:** "Blessed be the God and Father of our Lord Jesus Christ, who has blessed us with every spiritual blessing in the heavenly places in Christ" (Eph. 1:3).

+ **Grace:** "So you, my son, be strong in the grace that is in Christ Jesus" (2 Tim. 2:1).

+ **Completion:** "And you are complete in Him, who is the head of all authority and power" (Col. 2:10).

+ **Perfection:** "Whom we preach, warning everyone and teaching everyone in all wisdom, so that we may present them perfect in Christ Jesus" (Col. 1:28).

And there are many other verses revealing this "in Christ" insight. When you behold the fullness of the inheritance, it leaves you speechless—especially when you realize His greatest impartation, the promise of all promises, is eternal life (1 John 2:25).

BEAUTIFUL BOUNDARIES

Before any of this intense and immense revelation from the New Testament was available, David understood how profoundly powerful it was to be chosen of God. Pondering this state of blessedness, he came to a conclusion that we should all be able to echo at this point. As we survey the spiritual territory that now belongs to us because of our covenant with God, we should echo his choice words: "The lines have fallen for me in pleasant places; *indeed, I have a beautiful inheritance*" (Ps. 16:6, ESV).

DECLARE WHO YOU ARE IN CHRIST

I declare that I am an heir of God and a joint heir with Christ! I have inherited all that God is and all that God has. I share in the inheritance of the firstborn Son of God. In His great intercessory prayer over the church, Jesus has already prayed His Word, His glory, His perfection, His love, and His oneness with the Father into my life. He also declared when He walked on the earth that His joy, His peace, and His power belong to me. Therefore, by faith, I lay hold to my inheritance. I refuse to ask for things God has already given me. I am an heir of God. I have inherited grace, righteousness, wisdom, victory, and much more. I claim the manifestation of these gifts. In Jesus's name, amen!

Additional reading: Proverbs 3:35; Galatians 4:1–7; Colossians 1:12–13; Hebrews 9:15; 1 Peter 1:3–4

Chapter 40

HEIRS OF SALVATION

But to which of the angels, did He say at any time, "Sit
on My right hand until I make Your enemies Your
footstool?" Are they not all ministering spirits, sent forth
to minister for those who shall be *heirs of salvation*?
—**Hebrews 1:13–14, mkjv**

T HE WORD *SALVATION* is found 148 times in the Modern English Version of the Bible (104 times in the Old Testament and 44 times in the New Testament). It always means deliverance of some kind (not just from past sins). For instance, when the children of Israel stood at the edge of the Red Sea and Pharaoh's army was swiftly approaching, Moses declared:

> Stand still, and see *the salvation of the* Lord, which He will accomplish for you today. For the Egyptians whom you see today, you shall see again no more forever.
> —Exodus 14:13, nkjv

When Paul was incarcerated, he wrote to the Philippian church:

> For I know that this shall turn to *my salvation* through your prayer, and the supply of the Spirit of Jesus Christ.
> —Philippians 1:19, kjv

In both of these examples salvation meant something different than deliverance from sin. The children of Israel were delivered from a bloodbath at the hands of the Egyptian army. Paul was delivered from prison and from Jewish zealots who had been trying to kill him. For the "heirs of salvation" this word can mean a whole range of benefits, including deliverance from sin, from satanic plots, from the curse of Adam, from the curse of the law, and ultimately, from death, hell, and the grave. Yes, God has saved us or delivered us from all of these things.

The Threefold Nature of Salvation

We human beings have a triune nature: spirit, soul, and body. Parallel to this our salvation is also threefold:

+ We *were saved* from the penalty of sin when our spirits were regenerated and renewed in the Holy Spirit. (See Titus 3:5.)

+ We *are being saved* from the power of sin as we daily experience deliverance from soulish battles of the mind, will, and emotions. (See James 1:21; Philippians 2:12.)

+ We *will be saved* from the presence of sin when we are delivered from the bondage of our flesh, when the dead in Christ are raised, and living believers are translated at the coming of the Lord. (See Hebrews 9:28.)

God Our Savior

Under the old covenant salvation was primarily "of the Jews" (John 4:22). Now under the new covenant God "desires all men to be saved and to come to the knowledge of the truth" (1 Tim. 2:4). After Mary conceived of the Holy Spirit, the angel commanded Joseph, "You shall call His name JESUS, for He will save His people from their sins" (Matt. 1:21). How appropriate! For the name *Jesus* (in Hebrew, *Yeshua*) means "Yahweh is salvation," or "the salvation of Yahweh," or in essence "God manifested as a Savior."[1]

The same voice that insisted under the old covenant, "besides Me there is no Savior" (Isa 43:11) still states under the new covenant, "I am the door. If anyone enters through Me, he will be saved and will go in and out and find pasture" (John 10:9). The Yahweh of the Old Testament is the Jesus of the New Testament, and He still sends forth the urgent appeal: "Turn to Me, and be saved, all the ends of the earth. For I am God, and there is no other" (Isa. 45:22).

The Nature of Salvation

No one can earn salvation. It cannot be achieved by character development, religious works, or man-made rituals. We never become good enough to be saved. We simply reach out with faith, humility, and sincerity and gratefully receive what God delights to give. "For by grace you have been saved through faith, and this is not of yourselves. It is the gift of God, not of works, so that no one should boast" (Eph. 2:8–9).

Parents should expect this gift to be passed down to their offspring as well, for God's salvation is "from generation to generation" (Isa. 51:8). He has already promised, "I will contend with him who contends with you, and I will save your children" (Isa. 49:25, WEB; see also Luke 19:1–10).

Thank God, it's not difficult to be saved. Mysterious mystical formulas are not required. Years of self-abasement and self-discipline are not demanded to qualify. It is so utterly simple: "Whoever calls on the name of the Lord shall be saved" (Rom. 10:13).

THE MANY SIDES OF *SOZO*

The main Greek word translated "save" is *sozo*, found 110 times in the New Testament. Interestingly in the KJV it has also been translated "heal," "preserve," "made whole," and "do well."[2] In the NKJV it is rendered "get well" and "made well." In the RSV it is translated "recover."

Some specific examples include:

+ **The demoniac at Gadara:** "He who had been possessed by demons was *healed*" (Luke 8:36).

+ **Paul's expectation:** "The Lord will deliver me from every evil work and will *preserve* me for His heavenly kingdom, to whom be glory forever and ever. Amen" (2 Tim. 4:18).

+ **Jesus declaring to blind Bartemaeus:** "Go your way. Your faith has *made you well*" (Mark 10:52). (The KJV translates it as "whole.")

+ **The disciples said of Lazarus:** "Lord, if he sleeps he will *get well*" (John 11:12). (The RSV translates it as "recover.")

These four examples reveal that salvation is not just limited to forgiveness of sins; it involves healing, preservation, wellness, soundness, and wholeness in our entire being. It involves full recovery from personal failures, the fall of Adam, and every natural or spiritual limitation. James connects healing of the body and the soul with the promise:

> Is anyone sick among you? Let him call for the elders of the church, and let them pray over him, anointing him with oil in the name of the Lord. And the prayer of faith will save [Greek *sozo*] the sick, and the Lord will raise him up. And if he has committed any sins, he will be forgiven.
>
> —JAMES 5:14–15

Finally, Hebrews 7:25 states that Jesus is "able to save [Greek *sozo*] to the uttermost those who come to God through Him, because He at all times lives to make intercession for them."

ULTIMATE SALVATION

Thank God, the day will come when "all the ends of the earth shall see the salvation of our God" (Isa. 52:10). The saints will be gloriously transformed at the coming of the Lord. For those looking for His return, He shall "appear the second time without sin unto salvation" (Heb. 9:28, KJV). We will then be thrust into the next phase of God's purposes in this vast, magnificent universe.

When time will merge with eternity, what ecstasy will be ours as we join the white-robed, palm-waving throng on the sea of glass mingled with fire! Surrounded by the angels who helped us on our journey, we will joyously shout that ultimate declaration of triumph: "Salvation belongs to our God who sits on the throne, and to the Lamb!" (Rev. 7:10).

DECLARE WHO YOU ARE IN CHRIST

I declare that I am an heir of salvation! I declare that Jesus will save me to the uttermost, in every area of my being: body, soul, and spirit, for He ever lives to make intercession for me. I am saved from sin, from sickness, and from every satanic plot. Ultimately I will be saved from the clutches of death. Holy angels are constantly ministering deliverance to me in times of trouble. "What shall I render unto the Lord for all His benefits toward me? I will take the cup of salvation and call upon the name of the Lord" (Ps. 116:12–13).

The name Jesus means "the salvation of God"—so every time I utter His name, I am affirming the salvation covenant I have from Him. I am not saved by works; I am saved by grace, and this is the gift of God. In Jesus's name, amen!

Additional reading: Psalm 149:4; Isaiah 12:3; 45:17; 60:18; 62:1; Luke 18:18–27; John 12:47; Acts 4:12

Chapter 41

A HOLY NATION

But you are a chosen generation, a royal priesthood,
a holy nation, His own special people, that you
may proclaim the praises of Him who called you
out of darkness into His marvelous light.
—1 PETER 2:9, NKJV

THIS VERSE CELEBRATES the identity of God's new covenant offspring in jubilant terms. However, the language is very similar to a statement God made under the first covenant. Right before He manifested His glory on Mount Sinai, the Lord of hosts spoke through Moses to Israel:

> Now therefore, if you will indeed obey My voice and keep My covenant, then you shall be a special treasure to Me above all people; for all the earth is Mine. And you shall be to Me a kingdom of priests and *a holy nation*.
> —EXODUS 19:5–6, NKJV

So God's primary desire has always been the same. Even though His methods have drastically changed, He is still reaching for a similar end result—a truly devoted people, special to Him, who will walk in "the way of holiness" as they pass through this world to their eternal reward (Isa. 35:8, ESV).

UNDERSTANDING THE TERM

The word *holy* means to be set apart, separated from the world, and consecrated to God. It comes from a root that means to be whole or sound. So holiness is wholeness. Sin leaves people dysfunctional and fragmented. Holiness ushers them toward completion and fullness.

Holiness is one of the essential attributes of God. On one hand, it means freedom from all moral evil. On the other hand, it means the absolute of all that is morally good.

Therefore, everything associated with God is and must be holy. He is the "Holy Father" (John 17:11). His emanating presence is called the "Holy Spirit" (Ps. 51:11). His Word is referred to as "the Holy Scriptures" (2 Tim. 3:15). Romans 7:12 explains "the law is holy, and the commandment holy" (NKJV), and Psalm 105:42 speaks of "His holy promise." The tithe is even described as being "holy" (Lev. 27:30), and significant high places where God moved in remarkable ways are called "holy mountains" (Ps. 87:1, NKJV).

In the tabernacle of Moses the priests ministered in "the holy place" (Exod. 26:33). The high priest alone entered a chamber called the holy of holies, or the "Most Holy" (Exod. 26:33) one time a year on the Day of Atonement, which was set aside as a "holy convocation" for all God's people (Lev. 23:27). All the furniture and utensils in the tabernacle were described as "most holy" (Exod. 30:29). The altar offerings were called "holy gifts" (Exod. 28:38) and "holy sacrifices" (Ezek. 36:38, NKJV). The high priest wore "holy garments" (Exod. 29:29) and a turban bearing the inscription, "HOLINESS TO THE LORD" on a golden plate (Exod. 39:30). Everything pertaining to worship was anointed with "holy anointing oil" (Exod. 30:25).

Thirty times in the Old Testament God is referred to as "the holy One of Israel" (Ps. 71:22, KJV). He even names Himself and describes His dwelling place with this potent word:

> For thus says the High and Lofty One who inhabits eternity, *whose name is Holy*: "I dwell in *the high and holy place*, with him who has a contrite and humble spirit, to revive the spirit of the humble, and to revive the heart of the contrite ones."
> —ISAIAH 57:15, NKJV

So once again everything associated with God is, and must be, holy. Therefore, it is only to be expected that He commands His people: "Be holy, for I am holy" (Lev. 11:45; see also 1 Peter 1:16).

Of course, attaining that goal was far more challenging under the old covenant, for it was primarily based on human will and human effort.

THE MIRACLE OF THE NEW BIRTH

In the new covenant those who come to God are washed in the blood of Jesus—an experience Titus 3:5 called "the washing of regeneration" (NKJV) or "the washing of rebirth" (MEV). At that moment they are each infused with "a new spirit" that is pure, uncontaminated, and in the image of God (Ezek. 36:26). Then they should choose to be covered daily with the mind-set of this new man. (See Colossians 3:10.) Ephesians explains this more fully:

> For you ought to put off the old man (according to your way of living before) who is corrupt according to the deceitful lusts, and be renewed in the spirit of your mind. And you should put on the new man, who according to God was *created in righteousness and true holiness.*
> —EPHESIANS 4:22–24, MKJV

Why is this spiritual impartation called "true holiness"? Because it is not achieved externally through religious ceremonies and the keeping of rules; it is received internally—supernaturally created at the moment of spiritual rebirth.

Just as Jesus was "declared to be the Son of God with power according to the Spirit of holiness, by the resurrection from the dead" (Rom. 1:4), so we are confirmed as sons and daughters of God, by the Spirit of holiness raising us up from the state of being "dead in...trespasses and sins" (Eph. 2:1).

The outcome should still be the keeping of commandments (that hasn't changed—there are over one thousand in the New Testament alone). But the core reason and motivation has changed. Instead of being driven by the fear of failure and resulting judgments, Jesus's followers are simply urged, "If you love Me, keep My commandments" (John 14:15). Now our dominating passion should be to "worship the LORD in the beauty of holiness" (Ps. 29:2, NKJV).

STILL THE DIVINE MANDATE

Internal, Holy Spirit–birthed holiness is not an end in itself; it validates its existence by manifesting in external holiness. In other words, if you've got, you'll show it.

Besides, without holiness "no one will see the Lord" (Heb. 12:14).

In other words, to "see God" significantly manifest Himself in our own personal lives and to "see God" bring forth a spiritual awakening in our generation, we, the church, must separate ourselves from fleshly and worldly things that are displeasing to God.

With this in mind, the following New Testament exhortations are a good way of bringing this chapter to a close:

> I urge you therefore, brothers, by the mercies of God, that you present your bodies as a living sacrifice, *holy*, and acceptable to God, which is your reasonable service of worship. Do not be conformed to this world, but be transformed by the renewing of your mind.
>
> —Romans 12:1–2

> Since we have these promises, beloved, let us cleanse ourselves from all filthiness of the flesh and spirit, *perfecting holiness in the fear of God*.
>
> —2 Corinthians 7:1

> For God has not called us to uncleanness, but to *holiness*. Therefore he that despises does not despise man, but God, who has also given us His Holy Spirit.
>
> —1 Thessalonians 4:7–8

Declare Who You Are in Christ

I declare that I am part of a holy nation! When I was born again, my regenerated spirit—a new creation—was infused with the very holiness of God. For this reason I am victorious over the curse of the fallen nature. It is now my new nature to live holy. So I daily make the decision to "put on the new man, which after God is created in righteousness and true holiness" (Eph. 4:24, KJV). I present my body a "living sacrifice, holy, and acceptable to God" (Rom. 12:1). I claim the holiness of God ruling all of my decisions in life as I travel the "way of holiness" (Isa. 35:8, ESV) back to the holy Father who has given me His "holy promise" (Ps. 105:42). And on my journey I often shout, "Holy, holy, holy is the Lord of hosts, who was and is and is to come." In Jesus's name, amen!

Additional reading: Deuteronomy 7:6; 14:2; Isaiah 6:3; 1 Timothy 2:8; Revelation 4:8; 21:2

Chapter 42

KINGS

To Him who loved us and washed us from our
sins in His own blood, and has made us *kings*
and priests to His God and Father, to Him be
glory and dominion forever and ever. Amen.
—**REVELATION 1:5–6**

OLOMON SAID, "IT is the glory of God to conceal a thing, but
the honor of kings is to search out a matter" (Prov. 25:2). Since
God actually refers to His new covenant people as kings, this will be
a double honor for us—first, to search out the meaning of this regal
title, and second, to walk in the resulting revelation of our kingship
with boldness.

There is no better place to start than the song of Hannah. One
verse in that celebrated prayer always excites my heart and expands
my mind concerning God's great purposes for us: "He raises the
poor from the dust and lifts the beggar from the ash heap, to set
them among princes and make them inherit the throne of glory"
(1 Sam. 2:8, NKJV). The King James translates "from the ash heap"
as "from the dunghill." Here is a deeper explanation of this verse:

+ The word *poor* in this verse probably refers to more than
  just those who struggle materially. Most likely it also
  denotes those who are "poor in spirit," those who humbly
  recognize their bankrupt spiritual condition in Adam
  (Matt. 5:3).

+ The dust represents mortality. As Genesis 3:19 says, "*You
  are dust, and to dust you will return.*" So God delivers the
  poor in spirit from the "dust of mortality." That's the first
  promise.

- The word *beggar* refers to more than just needy individuals pleading for a handout. Most likely it alludes to those who humbly plead for mercy from God.

- The dunghill, or the ash heap, represents carnality (the fallen nature) and the destruction that results, for "to be carnally minded is death" (Rom. 8:6).

- So God delivers those who cry out to Him from the dunghill of carnality and its death-dealing influence. This is the second promise

But God doesn't just bring us out; He takes us in. The Most High lifts the "poor" from the grip of mortality and the "beggar" from the pit of carnality "to set them among princes." In other words, they become God's royal seed: sons of the King and heirs of His throne. No jostling for advantage is necessary, or palace intrigue, or evil plots, or murderous conspiracies—for unselfish love is the prevailing atmosphere of God's kingdom and besides, every one of His offspring inherit the status of a king. No competition is even necessary. (See Revelation 3:21.)

REIGNING NOW

Our key verse celebrates the One who "has made us kings and priests to His God and Father" (Rev. 1:6). Notice this statement is in the past tense—it does not say He *will*, but rather that He *has* given us this regal inheritance. So this is not just a futuristic promise pertaining to the government of God in a perfected paradise yet to come. We are kings right now—right here in this fallen world—in practical and powerful ways.

Jesus is the "KING OF KINGS" (Rev. 19:16), the "ruler of the kings of the earth" (Rev. 1:5). He reigns from heaven, but we are His earthly representatives, establishing His authority here. We are emissaries of God's kingdom, declaring His heaven-sent decrees that they might be known on earth. But that's not the only way we exhibit kingly dominion. It starts with evidence of restored "dominion" in our lives from the moment of salvation (Gen. 1:26).

Two precious gifts from God instantly transform us from being slaves to sin, groveling in the mire of our lost state, to reigning monarchs, overcoming this world: the gift of grace and the gift of righteousness. As Romans 5:17 says:

> For if by one man's trespass death reigned through him, then how much more will those who receive abundance of grace and the gift of righteousness reign in life through the One, Jesus Christ.[1]

There is no spiritual battle, no disappointment, no depressive circumstance, no satanic strategy, no failed relationship, no personal weakness, and no past failure that children of God cannot rise above victoriously by accessing the grace of God and by humbly acquiring "the righteousness which is of God by faith" (Phil. 3:9, kjv; see also Romans 5:2; 6:14; 10:10).

We also reign by manifesting kingdom character in all the negative things we encounter day by day. When people around us express characteristics of the kingdom of darkness, we are called to respond by exhibiting traits inherent to the kingdom of light:

- ✦ We reign over discouragement by manifesting hope.
- ✦ We reign over anger by speaking words of kindness.
- ✦ We reign over bitterness by flowing in forgiveness.
- ✦ We reign over skepticism by exhibiting faith.
- ✦ We reign over anxiety by promoting peace.
- ✦ We reign over pride by expressing humility.
- ✦ We reign over sensuality by walking in purity.
- ✦ We reign over selfishness by loving others with the love of God.

Yes, in these and hundreds of other ways, both subtle and blatant, we seize opportunities to establish our status as kings. You see, it's not about parading through some royal court in expensive attire before admiring eyes. It's not about ostentatious demonstrations of self-created grandeur.

The prototype—the firstborn Son of God—didn't look like a king. But He acted like one, in simple and humble ways.

And He is our example.

Reigning in the World to Come

This life is not an end in itself. This kingly calling has not been fully developed in us yet. We are presently training for reigning on a level far beyond our capacity to fully envision. Hannah summed it up by prophesying that we will "inherit the throne of glory" (1 Sam. 2:8). That's God's throne! That means sharing His authority as corulers over His vast domain and establishing His kingdom in a restored – paradise world! If God were to lift His royal seed any higher, it would intrude into the exclusive domain of the Godhead itself.

John predicted how the children of the kingdom will react to this divine benevolence when the Lamb of God takes the seven-sealed scroll from the Father and opens the portal to a new and spectacular era:

> When He had taken the scroll, the four living creatures and the twenty-four elders fell down before the Lamb, each one having a harp, and golden bowls full of incense, which are the prayers of saints. And they sang a new song, saying: "You are worthy to take the scroll, and to open its seals; for You were slain, and have redeemed us to God by Your blood out of every tribe and tongue and people and nation, and have made us *kings and priests unto our God*; and we shall reign on the earth."
>
> —Revelation 5:8–10

In that day, like the twenty-four elders, we will surely feel compelled to cast our crowns before the Redeemer God and declare with an innumerable throng of worshippers: "Worthy is the Lamb to receive the highest praise! May all the glory and honor and praise return to Him alone!"

Declare Who You Are in Christ

I declare that spiritually speaking I am a king! I am reigning with the Lord Jesus Christ right now, enthroned with Him in heavenly places, and manifesting His authority on the earth. By the grace of God and His gift of righteousness, I reign over sin, I reign over the flesh, I reign over the spirit of the world, and I reign over every satanic strategy against me. I have purposed that I will express kingly dominion wherever I go by manifesting the character of God's kingdom of light in my dealings with others. By doing so, I assist in conquering the kingdom of darkness and establishing the government of God in this world—all in preparation for that fully manifested dominion which is yet to come. In Jesus's name, amen!

Additional reading: Genesis 17:1–6; Psalm 8:4–6; Isaiah 32:1; Daniel 7:27; 1 Corinthians 4:8; Revelation 20:4–6

Chapter 43

MORE THAN CONQUERORS

No, in all these things we are *more than conquerors* through Him who loved us.
—ROMANS 8:37

To be a conqueror is to overcome some opposition or challenge by personal strength. To be "more than a conqueror" is to overcome through the efforts of another, to win by association, or to receive benefits through the price that someone else pays.

When the United States forces stormed Normandy on June 6, 1944, against the fierce opposition of the German army, miraculously, by the help of God, they emerged as conquerors. But the populace of the United States who lived within the safe confines of our nation's peaceful boundaries instantly became more than conquerors. They won through the intense efforts of those unselfish heroes who threw themselves on a blood-soaked beachhead and crawled forward under heavy machine gun fire.

In like manner Jesus faced fierce, hellish attacks against His Messianic claims, but He pushed through the opposition and conquered all the archenemies of the human race. Though torturously crucified, He emerged the conqueror, "triumphing over them by the cross" (Col. 2:15). However, we who covenant with Him do not just become conquerors; we emerge as more than conquerors—because it was not through our efforts but through His grappling with the foes of humanity that we are able to overcome all things.

THE SUPREMACY OF LOVE

To fully understand this revelation, it is best that we read it in context:

> Who shall separate us from the love of Christ? Shall tribulation, or distress, or persecution, or famine, or nakedness, or

peril, or sword? As it is written: "For your sake we are killed all day long; we are counted as sheep for the slaughter." No, in all these things we are *more than conquerors* through Him who loved us. For I am persuaded that neither death nor life, neither angels nor principalities nor powers, nor things present nor things to come, neither height nor depth, nor any other created thing, shall be able to separate us from the love of God which is in Christ Jesus our Lord.

—Romans 8:35–39

So the key element in seizing this portion of our identity is comprehending the great love that God has bestowed upon His people and being convinced that nothing can separate us from that love. This is one of my favorite passages on this subject:

The Lord has appeared of old to me, saying: "Yes, I have loved you with an everlasting love; therefore with lovingkindness I have drawn you."

—Jeremiah 31:3, nkjv

An everlasting love has no beginning and no end, so there was never a point when God "started" loving you. In fact, being in love with you has always been a part of God. Even before you existed in this world, God's heart was consumed with His plans for you—so He draws you that direction every day with His kindness.

Intercession Over You

Both Jesus and the Holy Spirit have interceded over you, that you would have a love encounter that would transform you forever. In John 17, just before He went into Gethsemane, Jesus prayed over the church that would yet be birthed. (I suggest you read the whole prayer, beginning in verse 1.) At the end of this time of intercession He petitioned:

Father, I desire that they also, whom You have given Me, be with Me where I am, that they may see My glory which You have given Me. For *You loved Me before the creation of the world.* O righteous Father, the world has not known You, but I have known You, and these have known that You sent Me. I have declared Your name to them, and will declare it, *that the love with which You loved Me may be in them*, and I in them.

—JOHN 17:24–26

Can you fathom the depth of that declaration? Jesus prayed we would be filled with the same love that the Father felt for Him. Amazing! That incomparable love rested upon Him before His incarnation; it preserved Him in His great trial, and it powerfully propelled Him through *Sheol* (the Hebrew word for the grave and the underworld) to glory and victory. What an unconquerable, unbreakable bond between Him and the Father! And will it not be the same for you?

Later on the Holy Spirit inspired the following prayer in the writings of Paul:

> That Christ may dwell in your hearts through faith; that you, *being rooted and grounded in love*, may be able to comprehend with all saints what is the breadth and length and depth and height, and to *know the love of Christ which surpasses knowledge*; that you may be filled with all the fullness of God.
>
> —EPHESIANS 3:17–19

You need to vocally declare right now, "I receive that prayer. I accept all of that into my life right now." How can you say that? Because that wasn't just Paul praying for the Ephesian church, that was the Holy Spirit praying through Paul for the entire church—including you and me. And when the Son of God or the Holy Spirit prays, without fail, the Father answers. (See 2 Timothy 3:16; Romans 8:26–27).[1]

Several things grab my heart concerning Ephesians 3:17–19:

+ First, we must be "rooted and grounded in love" in order to comprehend the vastness of God's plan.

+ Second, this love "surpasses knowledge," so it must be supernaturally experienced in the heart; it cannot be understood intellectually, even with an abundance of theological terms.

+ Third, only when this love is revealed in you can you be "filled with all the fullness of God."

Jesus's two great commandments of the new covenant—loving God with all your heart and loving your neighbor as yourself—are far more profound and powerful than the Ten Commandments of the old covenant. (See Matthew 22:36–40.) In fact, love is what began the new covenant (meditate awhile on John 3:16: "For God so loved the world…"). Love is the essence of the new covenant and an even greater revelation of love will be its outcome, when the Lord of love returns. The highly symbolic book Song of Songs ends with the bride coming out of the wilderness, leaning on the arm of her beloved, as she pleads:

> Set me as a seal upon your heart…for love is strong as death.…Many waters cannot quench love, neither can the floods drown it.
>
> —Song of Songs 8:6–7

That really is the conclusion of the whole matter—though the enemy came in like a flood, in all of our lives, it could not quench the fire of God's love for us, nor our love for Him. And for that reason, above all others, we are and ever will be "more than conquerors."

Declare Who You Are in Christ

I declare that I am more than a conqueror through Him who loved me! When Jesus went to the cross, He had me in mind. He loved me then and He loves me now—and nothing can separate me from His everlasting love. As long as I respond to the Savior of the world in faith, humility, and sincere love, I am unconquerable in all things. No matter what I face in life, I will emerge victorious, one way or the other. By the help of God, I will even conquer the greatest challenge to be faced in this world—death itself. The Father's love prevailed for Jesus and brought Him out of the grave; it will prevail eternally for me as well. In Jesus's name, amen!

Additional reading: Deuteronomy 7:6–8; Zephaniah 3:17; John 15:9; 1 John 3:1 (kjv)

Chapter 44

OVERCOMERS

'And I shall grant the *overcomer* to sit with
me on my throne, just as I have overcome
and I sit with my Father on his throne.
—**REVELATION 3:21,** ABPE

T O OVERCOME MEANS to rise above, to conquer, to defeat, to prevail over, to overpower, or to overwhelm. It always means to be "over" something or someone, exerting dominion or forcing submission.

In his revered, ancient treatise on military strategy titled *The Art of War,* famed Chinese general Sun Tzu taught that an army should never attack an enemy on higher ground. Unfortunately prior to our salvation the enemy of the human race—the prince of this world—*was* on higher ground spiritually. This "accuser" occupied a position of authority over all the offspring of Adam, because of our fallen, degraded, and sin-stained condition (Rev. 12:10).

Thank God, all of this shifted dramatically when we accepted Jesus as Lord of our lives. Because He has been exalted "far above" all things and all things are "under his feet," when we entered a covenant with Him, we were immediately escorted to this same place of superiority and supremacy (Eph. 1:21–22). So initially being an overcomer is an inherited position. As soon as we submit to the One on the throne, all things are under our feet as well. (See 1 Corinthians 15:28.) Such a magnificent legacy will do us little good, though, unless we seize it by faith, speak it with boldness and walk in its reality every day of our lives.

OUR SOURCE OF OVERCOMING POWER

The first step is developing the mind-set of an overcomer. There is no better example than Caleb's attitude toward the ten spies who brought back a negative report concerning the Promised Land. With fear-filled hearts and trembling voices, they spoke about the prospect of fighting giants and the impossibility of managing such a large land mass, but Caleb's penetrating words were like polished arrows shot from a spiritual bow: "Let us go up at once and possess it, for we are well able to overcome it" (Num. 13:30).

His assessment was not based on human logic, but on revelation and faith. He knew they had been commissioned to occupy the land of promise by the plan of the almighty God and that was enough to predetermine the outcome, regardless of the odds. It finally happened forty years later because of his tenacious faith, along with his confident comrade, Joshua. In their day they overcame in four main ways: by divine inspiration, divine empowerment, divine intervention, and the divine commitment to reverse every curse that came against God's people. (See Deuteronomy 23:5; Romans 8:28.) We can expect the same kind of assistance and outcome, for we are a part of a plan that cannot be defeated.

Jesus understood these things very well, so He dared to announce to His disciples in the past tense, "I have overcome the world" (John 16:33). He spoke of ultimate victory as if it had already taken place, even before He faced the cross and the tomb. He spoke with absolute confidence, as if He had already emerged triumphant. Because in the mind of the Father, the victory had already been secured. God's plan from the beginning dictated that He be loosed from the grips of death, "because it was not possible that He should be held by it" (Acts 2:24).

We can have just as great an assurance concerning all that we might face in our future. Notice the following passages speak to us in the past tense also:

> I have written to you, young men, because you are strong, and the word of God lives in you, and *you have overcome the evil one.*
> —1 JOHN 2:14

> Beloved, do not believe every spirit, but test the spirits to see whether they are from God.... You are of God, little children, and *have overcome them,* because He who is in you is greater than he who is in the world.
> —1 JOHN 4:1, 4

For whatever is born of God overcomes the world. And this is the victory that *has overcome the world*—our faith.

—1 John 5:4, nkjv; see also 1 John 2:27

These three passages of Scripture have one primary thing in common. They declare that we already *have overcome*—even before we wrestle with any demonic attacks or negative circumstances that may yet arise in our future. Four primary reasons are given:

+ The written Word of God abides in us. The truth in us is far more powerful than any evil maneuverings outside of us—so Satan is already a conquered foe.

+ Jesus, the living Word, abides in us. He is far more powerful than any evil spirits plotting against us—so all demonic devices against us are already defeated.

+ We have been born again (spiritually regenerated) so the Spirit of God now abides in us. This automatically exalts believers above every adversary and negative circumstance we face in life.

+ Finally, we believe in the covenant we have with God. All of this works simply because we have faith.

In a sense we all have a spiritual promised land to possess as well. It is comprised of all the written Word promises made to the entire church, as well as personal living Word promises God has made to us as individuals. We know God keeps His promises; therefore, let us declare in Caleb-like fashion:

> We are well able to overcome this world! We are well able fulfill our calling, to reign in life and to emerge victorious from death. For we have weapons of warfare that are mighty through God. Let us go up at once and seize our purpose in the Lord, fulfilling the perfect will of God and accomplishing all the good we possibly can while passing through this world.

The Rewards

In the Book of the Revelation eighteen rewards are promised to those who overcome (such as eating of the tree of life, partaking of hidden manna, wearing a crown of life, and inheriting all things). Of all of them, probably the most spectacular is the promise featured at the beginning of this chapter, our Savior's declaration:

> And I shall grant the *overcomer* to sit with me on my throne, just as I have overcome and I sit with my Father on his throne.
> —REVELATION 3:21, ABPE

To share the very throne of God—what an amazing thought! To partake of His authority, reigning with the King of kings over a perfected new creation—what a powerful prophetic glimpse into our future destiny! Yet this is not only a futuristic promise. We are enthroned with the Lord right now—for God has "raised us up and seated us together in the heavenly places in Christ Jesus" (Eph. 2:6). So technically speaking, from the very moment of our salvation, we are not just those who aspire *to be overcomers* someday. Rather, we *are overcomers*—right here, right now!

DECLARE WHO YOU ARE IN CHRIST

I declare that I am an overcomer! Because the written Word of God abides in me, I have already overcome the evil one. Because Jesus abides in me, I have already overcome all demonic powers and their plots against me. No weapon formed against me shall prosper. Because of my faith, I have already overcome the world and any negative thing that I might ever face in life, even death. I declare that I have a purpose in God; this is my personal promised land. I will overcome all opposition and I will possess it. In Jesus's name, amen!

Additional reading: 2 Corinthians 2:14; Romans 8:35–39; Revelation 2:7, 10–11, 17, 26–28; 3:5, 12; 21:7

PART 7

YOU ARE DESTINED

Chapter 45

CHILDREN OF THE RESURRECTION

And Jesus answering said unto them, The children of
this world marry, and are given in marriage: but they
which shall be accounted worthy to obtain that world,
and the resurrection from the dead, neither marry,
nor are given in marriage: Neither can they die any
more: for they are equal unto the angels; and are the
children of God, being the *children of the resurrection.*
—LUKE 20:34–36, KJV

JESUS SPOKE THESE words to a group of skeptical Sadducees intent
on challenging the doctrine of the resurrection. They related the
story of a woman who was married to seven brothers (one after the
other), all of whom died. Grasping for a logical explanation, they
asked, "In the resurrection whose wife will she be? For the seven
had her as a wife" (Luke 20:33). Jesus then gave the response above.

Notice the Savior never indicated children of God will be gen-
derless in the future state; He simply said that we will not marry.
Glorified saints will most likely maintain the appearance of male or
female according to their previous earthly identities, but marriage
and reproduction will no longer be a part of how things function in
the eternal, glorified state.

THE ORIGINAL DILEMMA

The Greek word translated "resurrection" in our primary passage is
anastasis, meaning a standing up again.[1] It can also mean a moral
recovery.

That's what we needed. Adam and Eve walked into the gaping
mouth of death in the very beginning and passed on that state of
spiritual, mental, emotional, and physical death to all their offspring.

All human beings are born "dead in trespasses and sins" (Eph. 2:1). Because of our fallen nature (prior to salvation), choices in life far too often are ruled by lust (selfish desire). This always results in a horrid chain of events, dictated by the inexorable rule that governs this realm called "the law of sin and death" (Rom. 8:2). James defined this law succinctly: "Then, when lust has conceived, it brings forth sin; and when sin is finished, it brings forth death" (James 1:15).

Being born into this realm is like stepping in spiritual quicksand. No matter how hard we fight against it, the grip of death keeps pulling us under. But then that pivotal moment comes when the Savior stands outside the tomb of our troubled lives (just as He did with Lazarus) and speaks words filled with hope: "I am the resurrection and the life. He who believes in Me, though he may die, yet shall he live" (John 11:25).

What a blessing to know the answer to the human dilemma! Acting on Romans 10:8–10, we believed in our hearts that God raised Jesus from the dead and we confessed with our lips, accepting the Messiah as Lord of our lives. It worked. We were saved. We were resurrected spiritually, revived, brought back to life, raised from the dead mentally and emotionally. God even gave us a brand-new spirit infused with the gift of everlasting life. There are no words to sufficiently describe the power of this promise.

Now the goal is continuing the process, knowing Him in "the power of His resurrection" on a daily basis (Phil. 3:10). "Even though our outward man is perishing, yet our inward man is being renewed"—resurrected, restored, made new, lifted up into victory, every moment of every day (2 Cor. 4:16). Even if we go through heartbreaking disappointments, we can adamantly shout aloud as the Prophet Micah did: "Do not rejoice over me, my enemy; when I fall, I will arise" (Mic. 7:8, NKJV).

Through it all we are looking forward to that grand moment when the Lord will complete His resurrection work in us on the "last day" of this age (John 6:39–40). There are many powerful passages that describe this grand event:

> Listen, I tell you a mystery: We shall not all sleep, but we shall all be changed. In a moment, in the twinkling of an eye, at

the last trumpet, for the trumpet will sound, the dead will be raised incorruptible, and we shall be changed.

—1 CORINTHIANS 15:51–52

But our citizenship is in heaven, from where also we await for our Savior, the Lord Jesus Christ, who will transform our body of humiliation, so that it may be conformed to His glorious body, according to the working of His power even to subdue all things to Himself.

—PHILIPPIANS 3:20–21

For the Lord Himself will descend from heaven with a shout, with the voice of the archangel, and with the trumpet call of God. And the dead in Christ will rise first. Then we who are alive and remain shall be caught up together with them in the clouds to meet the Lord in the air. And so we shall be forever with the Lord.

—1 THESSALONIANS 4:16–17

I believe of all the scriptures dealing with the resurrection of the dead or the translation of living believers at the return of Jesus, 1 John 3:2 is one of my favorites:

Beloved, now are we children of God, and it has not yet been revealed what we shall be. But we know that when He appears, we shall be like Him, for we shall see Him as He is.

Years ago I was meditating on this passage, and the Spirit of God spoke to my heart a number of the primary ways it will be fulfilled. Seven of the most powerful are:

- We shall be like Him in authority. (See Psalm 8:4–6; Revelation 3:21.)
- We shall be like Him in intelligence. (See John 15:15; 1 Corinthians 2:16; 13:12.)
- We shall be like Him in emotional capacity. (See John 14:27; 15:11; 17:26.)
- We shall be like Him in perfection. (See John 17:23.)
- We shall be like Him in supernatural abilities. (See John 14:26.)

- We shall be like Him in oneness with the Father. (See John 17:20–21.)
- We shall be like Him in appearances. (See Matthew 13:43, Revelation 1:16.)

On that day when God finally presents us "faultless before the presence of His glory," He will do so with "exceeding joy" (Jude 1:24, NKJV). If that be true, we should experience this triumphant kind of rejoicing even now, as we anticipate such a glorious future.

DECLARE WHO YOU ARE IN CHRIST

I declare that I am a child of the resurrection! I was dead in trespasses and sins, but God raised me up with the Lord Jesus and gave me the gift of eternal life. Now that I am saved, no death-dealing situations I face in life will ever prevail against me. By faith I declare that I will always rise victorious through the power of Jesus's resurrection working in my heart and life. Though the outer man perishes, the inward man is being renewed day by day, and moment by moment. I look forward to that grand event at the end of this age when the dead in Christ will arise in His likeness, and we who are alive will be caught up to meet the Lord in the air, glorified in a moment, in the twinkling of an eye. In Jesus's name, amen!

Additional reading: Deuteronomy 25:5–10; Luke 20:27–40; John 5:24–29; Revelation 20:4–6

Chapter 46

CHILDREN OF ZION

*Let Israel rejoice in its Maker; let the children
of Zion be joyful in their King.*
—Psalm 149:2

IN THE BEGINNING Zion was a ridge in southeast Jerusalem where David's tabernacle was erected to house the ark of the covenant after its return from the Philistines. (See 1 Chronicles 15–16; 2 Samuel 6.) As they gathered to the top of Mount Zion, the Israelite people arrived at a pivotal prophetic point because a grand departure from the Mosaic order had taken place there. David, by divine revelation, instituted a fresh approach to the worship of God:

+ **The ark in full view:** Instead of the ark being hidden behind a veil, to be seen only one day a year by the high priest on the Day of Atonement, apparently, though it may have had a covering, it was placed in the full view of all the priests and Levites who ministered daily before the Lord. God's glory must have radiated from His resting place on the mercy seat as constant praise ascended toward His throne—an acknowledgment that the tablets of stone the ark contained were to be honored and received. We can only imagine the awe-inspiring holiness and supernatural intensity of the atmosphere.

+ **Spiritual worship:** At its dedication, animal sacrifices were offered up, consecrating David's tabernacle, but never again afterward. Instead of a daily reminder of "sin and death" (Rom. 8:2), which was the normal pattern at Moses's tabernacle, the priests and the people of God gathered 24/7 to offer "spiritual sacrifices" (1 Pet. 2:5). This included sacrifices of righteousness, thanksgiving, praise, and joy—shouting, singing, dancing before the Lord, and playing the "instruments of God" (1 Chron. 16:42, NKJV; see also Psalms 4:5; 27:6; 47:1; 116:17; 149:3; Hebrews 13:15).

+ **The throne of the king:** David also erected a second tabernacle on Mount Zion housing his throne. Petitioners came to him there to present their cases and receive the king's just decrees.

The word *Zion* probably means citadel or fortress.[1] So when worshippers ascended the mountain called Zion, in a sense they were entering a fortress of faith in a world full of doubt, a fortress of hope in a world full of despair, a fortress of truth in a world full of deception. They approached *the throne of the king* and entered the atmosphere of *the glory of God*. What a fitting symbol for saints in the new covenant who prayerfully approach the throne of the King of all kings and are granted access into His glory. In fact, that is exactly what the word *Zion* represents now—it speaks of a glorious, heavenly realm, the high place of worship, that all of God's people ascend to worldwide—a place where we reign with Christ over all the negative things we face in this world.

In comparing the old and new covenants, the writer of Hebrews alluded to this spiritual reality by comparing the visitation at Mount Sinai to what happened on Mount Zion. To all New Testament believers he asserted:

> You have not come to the mountain that can be touched and that burned with fire, and to blackness and darkness and storm.... *But you have come to Mount Zion* and to the city of the living God, the heavenly Jerusalem, and to an innumerable company of angels; to the general assembly and church of the firstborn, who are enrolled in heaven; to God, the Judge of all; and to the spirits of the righteous ones made perfect; and to Jesus, the Mediator of a new covenant; and to the sprinkled blood that speaks better than that of Abel.
>
> —HEBREWS 12:18, 22–24

When we experienced the new birth, in a spiritual sense we became children of Zion—the offspring of a heavenly city, destined to walk within its confines forever. (See Psalm 87:5–6.) We did not find wholeness by coming to the law. We found grace, forgiveness, and restoration by approaching the throne of the great King, heaven's mediator, who pardoned us and allowed us to partake of His majesty. The early church understood that what transpired at the tabernacle of David was prophetic of the glory of the new covenant. (See Amos 9:11; Acts 15:16.)

Now in this era we can live on the slopes of this spiritual mountain every moment of every day, constantly praising and communing with God. It's not about rules and regulations. It's not about religion. We are all firstborn sons basking in the glorious love of our heavenly Father, enjoying the privileges of a "better covenant…established on better promises" (Heb. 8:6).

What powerful prophetic glimpses the seers, Jeremiah and Isaiah, shared concerning this blessed era:

> "In those days and in that time," says the LORD, "The children of Israel shall come, they and the children of Judah together; with continual weeping they shall come, and seek the LORD their God. They shall ask the way to Zion, with their faces toward it, saying, 'Come and let us join ourselves to the LORD in a perpetual covenant that will not be forgotten.'"
> —JEREMIAH 50:4–5, NKJV

> Therefore, the redeemed of the Lord shall return and come with singing to Zion, and everlasting joy shall be upon their head. They shall obtain gladness and joy, and sorrow and mourning shall flee away.
> —ISAIAH 51:11

This may all be wonderful now, but it's going to get even better. One day Zion will be the hub of the fully manifested government of God when His kingdom arrives in fullness and the Son of God reigns—in a spectacular era when "the earth will be filled with the knowledge of the glory of the LORD, as the waters cover the seas" (Hab. 2:14). In that day more than ever before "out of Zion, the perfection of beauty, God will shine forth" (Ps. 50:2, NKJV).

DECLARE WHO YOU ARE IN CHRIST

I declare that I am one of the children of Zion! I have approached the throne of the Lord and He has forgiven me. My sins have been washed away in the precious blood of Jesus and now I am part of the church of the firstborn. My name is written in heaven and in all the pressures and dis-appointments of life, I have a Mediator who is just and all – powerful. I am surrounded by an innumerable company of angels on my journey from time to eternity. I have found the fortress of faith in a world full of doubt, a fortress of love in a world full of hate. I have determined to live on the slopes of Mount Zion and worship God with every breath I breathe, for the rest of my days. In Jesus's name, amen!

Additional reading: 2 Samuel 5:4–10; 1 Chronicles 15–16; Psalms 2:1–12; 20:1–2; 50:1–3; Amos 9:11 (NKJV); Acts 15:16

Chapter 47

A CHOSEN GENERATION

But you are *a chosen generation*, a royal priesthood,
a holy nation, His own special people, that you
may proclaim the praises of Him who called you
out of darkness into His marvelous light.
—1 PETER 2:9, NKJV

THE WORD GENERATION can be defined four main ways:

+ An entire group of individuals born and living about the same time or during the same era
+ A group of individuals who share similar ideas or goals
+ The offspring of a certain parent
+ The act or the process of generating

The church from the Day of Pentecost onward can all claim being a part of the same generation because we are all part of the same era (the age of grace), we share similar ideas (such as Jesus's crucifixion being the key to salvation), and we are all descendants of the same progenitor (the Father of all creation). We may not be contemporaries naturally with the hundred and twenty who were in the Upper Room the day the Holy Spirit first fell, but we are supernaturally.

Psalm 22 confirms this truth. David first foretold the terrible, torturous treatment the Messiah would receive, even describing how they would pierce His hands and feet, but then he said, "A seed shall serve Him; it shall be accounted to the Lord for *a generation*" (Ps. 22:30, KJV).

That prophecy stretches across two millennia. All who accept Jesus as Lord are still part of the same generation. We are all the "seed" who serve the One who died in our place.

Isaiah 53 also gives detailed descriptions of the crucifixion. The prophet predicted the Messiah would be "despised and rejected of men…wounded for our transgressions…and by his stripes we are healed" (Isa. 53:3–5). Then he posed the question: "Who shall declare *his generation?*" (Isa. 53:8).

In other words, who will unveil the mystery of the new covenant family of God—the "chosen generation" spanning hundreds of years—that will result from this sacrifice? Those who understand are vitally important to God's cause, for He is depending on them to invite the people of the world to become a part of this spiritual family.

Psalm 24 pulls back the prophetic veil even further, first describing the ascension of the Lord Jesus into the heavenly holy of holies, then the covenant people who would result, saying: "This is *the generation* of those who seek Him, who seek Your face, O God of Jacob. Selah" (Ps. 24:6, MKJV).

So, according to these key passages, through the death of the Son of God, there will emerge a chosen, spiritual generation who will both "serve" and "seek" the God of Abraham, Isaac, and Jacob and who will "declare" the plan of salvation to this world.

WHO DOES GOD CHOOSE?

The answer to this question, quite often, is not what appears logical. Carefully read this passage explaining why God chose Israel under the old covenant:

> For you are a holy people to the LORD your God. The LORD your God has chosen you to be His special people, treasured above all peoples who are on the face of the earth. The LORD did not set His love on you nor choose you because you were more in number than any of the peoples, for you were the fewest of all the peoples. But it is because the LORD loved you and because He kept the oath which He swore to your fathers.
> —DEUTERONOMY 7:6–8

Instead of picking the most promising candidate for headship among the nations, God singled out the group least likely to succeed on their own, and then He implemented a plan spanning centuries that would evolve toward the fulfillment of His purpose. Doesn't that show what a mighty God He is?

Here's another great example from Acts 1:15–26. The early disciples felt that they needed to replace Judas, so at Peter's urging, they picked two men—Joseph (called Barsabas) and Matthias—and asked God to indicate which one was His choice. Their stipulation? They decided among themselves that it had to be a person who had been with them from the beginning. Lots were cast and Matthias was chosen. However, we are not told in Scripture that God actually led them to do this. Though Matthias was surely a good man (and there are traditions that claim he was used in the miraculous[1]), I believe God's choice for the twelfth apostle may have been someone else, possibly the very one least likely to fill such an honorable role.

A man named Saul, zealous to keep Judaism free of apostasy, "ravaged the church, entering house by house and dragging out both men and women and committing them to prison" (Acts 8:3). However, in the next chapter we find Jesus revealing Himself to Saul in a spectacular encounter on the road to Damascus, changing his name to Paul, and then telling Ananias: "This man is a chosen vessel of Mine, to bear My name before the Gentiles and their kings, and before the sons of Israel" (Acts 9:15). Later Paul confessed being an "apostle to the Gentiles" who was "born at the wrong time" (Rom. 11:13; 1 Cor. 15:8).

Can anybody shout, "Hallelujah!" Man's requirements are not always God's requirements. He doesn't always call the qualified; but He always qualifies the called. Many years later Paul shared what seems to be a divine pattern behind this whole process:

> For observe your calling, brothers. Among you, not many wise men according to the flesh, not many mighty men, and not many noble men were called. But God has chosen the foolish things of the world to confound the wise. God has chosen the weak things of the world to confound the things which are mighty. And God has chosen the base things of the world and things which are despised. Yes, and He chose things which did not exist to bring to nothing things that do, so that no flesh should boast in His presence.
>
> —1 Corinthians 1:26–29

God doesn't always choose rejects and outcasts. He doesn't always pick the unqualified. He also chooses intellectual, influential, and successful people. But still, it is encouraging to know that the criteria He goes by differ greatly from what this world thinks are necessary ingredients for success.

WHEN DOES GOD CHOOSE?

There is no more powerful way of answering this question than to quote Ephesians 1:4: "Just as He chose us in Him before the foundation of the world, to be holy and blameless before Him in love."

So believers are part of a plan that stretches from eternity past to eternity future. The big question, of course, is whether or not that plan predetermined that we be saved or was the product of foreknowledge on God's part. Regardless, knowing that we were in the mind of the Creator before we even got here should impart to us an amazing sense of assurance. Because the God who started a work in us will surely finish it.

WHY DID GOD CHOOSE?

This final question is easy to answer. Jesus told His closest disciples: "You have not chosen Me, but I have chosen you and ordained you that you should go and bring forth fruit, and that your fruit should remain" (John 15:16, MKJV).

Bearing eternal fruit in this temporal world is God's purpose for all His chosen ones. We must each follow His perfect will for our lives to be most effective and most productive. And remember—no one can do the job you are chosen to do better than you. You are God's best choice for the purpose He plants in your life.

DECLARE WHO YOU ARE IN CHRIST

I declare that I am part of a chosen generation! I am a member of the same spiritual generation that included all the early disciples, for we all claim the same heavenly Father. I declare that I did not choose Him, but He chose me and ordained me. He put my life in divine order and His main purpose is that I bear much fruit for the Father's glory. My commitment to the God who has chosen me is to gratefully choose His perfect will for my life and to abide in it faithfully all of my days. In Jesus's name, amen!

Additional reading: Psalm 33:12; Isaiah 41:8–10; Zechariah 3:2; Matthew 20:1–16; 22:1–14; Revelation 17:14

Chapter 48

AN EVERLASTING FOUNDATION

As the whirlwind passes, so the wicked is no more:
but the righteous is an everlasting foundation.
*—*Proverbs 10:25, kjv2000

WHEN A TORNADO (a whirlwind) passes through an area, the only proof of its temporary existence is the destruction it leaves behind—broken buildings, uprooted trees, injured people, and at times, those who are killed. So it is with those who live wicked lives. They pass through this world temporarily only to leave destruction everywhere they go—broken hearts, damaged lives, and a death-dealing effect on others, both mentally and emotionally.

Not so with the righteous. Their lives—full of godly principles, spiritual fruit, and purposeful goals—leave behind a strong foundation on which others can build. Children trying to find their way in life can build on the foundation of godly parents who walked in the truth before their impressionable eyes. Friends and coworkers who are seeking spiritual answers can build on the foundation of sincere Christians who live lives of integrity, honesty, fidelity, and responsibility in their midst. Even God Himself chooses to build His infinite plans and purposes on the lives of those who are faithfully committed to His cause.

The King James 2000 translates Proverbs 10:25 as "the righteous *is* an everlasting foundation," but the Modern English Version (our primary source) instead offers that, "the righteous *has* an everlasting foundation." Actually both renderings have relevance. Because the primary reason righteous individuals can *be* an everlasting foundation is because they *have* an everlasting foundation on which to build their lives.

There are only a few things revealed in Scripture that God cannot do, and one of them is that He cannot change. He even declared, "I am the Lord, I do not change" (Mal. 3:6). When we enter a covenant relationship with the God of Abraham, this unchangeable God offers at least eight stable, foundational things on which we can build our hopes and dreams. As you inspect the successive foundations, you will notice they keep increasing in size and scope as you go down the list:

- **Our own works of righteousness:** Righteous thoughts, righteous words, and righteous deeds are fertile ground for lasting fruit to grow in believers' lives. Of course, we cannot take credit for these good choices for God has "wrought all our works in us" (Isa. 26:12, KJV). Paul encouraged Timothy to tell those who are rich in this world's goods to be "rich in good works…laying up in store for themselves a good foundation for the coming age" (1 Tim. 6:18–19). And so it is for all of us. The righteous things we do today are laying a foundation for us to build on tomorrow.

- **Imparted righteousness:** Our good works cannot earn eternal life for us, but God has granted believers something far more powerful than humanly attained righteousness. It is called "the gift of righteousness" (Rom. 5:17). When we invite the Son of God into our hearts, He fills us with His own righteousness (Matt. 5:6). On this foundation of imparted righteousness we build a life full of works of righteousness.

- **The Word of God:** Hebrews 6:1–2 talks about "the foundation of repentance from dead works and of faith toward God, of the doctrine of baptisms, of laying on of hands, of resurrection of the dead, and of eternal judgment" (NKJV). But these six basic doctrines in Scripture are not the only foundational truths on which we are placing our trust. The entire Word of God is "the rock" on which we are building our hopes for the future (Matt. 7:24–25, NKJV).

- **The church:** Beneath the Word of God is the support structure of the entire church of God worldwide, a megalithic body of believers who uphold the Word even in times of opposition. The church is "the pillar and foundation of the truth," a bulwark against deception, a major support, from generation to generation, for all who love the truth (1 Tim. 3:15).

+ **The apostles and the prophets:** In Ephesians 2:19–20 the epistle writer shared how "the household of God" (the church) is "built upon the foundation of the apostles and prophets." Apostolic and prophetic ministries have connected heaven and earth and undergirded the church with such revelation that the "gates of Hades" will never "prevail against it" (Matt. 16:18). In the twelve foundations of the eternal city, New Jerusalem, are inscribed the names of the twelve apostles of the Lamb, for the success of the entire new covenant era rests on the foundation of their initial efforts (Rev. 21:14).

+ **God's holy mountains:** Psalm 87:1 claims, "God's foundation is in the holy mountains" (isv). The most significant spiritual events that have ever taken place in this world happened on mountains, such as Ararat, Moriah, Sinai, Hor, Nebo, Gerizim, Olivet, Calvary, and Zion. God laid the foundation of all that He is doing in the realm of time on these mountains, and they provide the unchanging, immoveable base and support of every true believer.

+ **God's foundational plan:** All that has transpired to redeem the human race was part of a foundational plan in the very beginning. Jesus was "the Lamb…slain from the foundation of the world" (Rev. 13:8). God's "works were finished from the foundation of the world" (Heb. 4:3, nkjv). One day we will enter a kingdom "prepared" for us from "the foundation of the world" (Matt. 25:34); all this is because "He chose us in Him before the foundation of the world" (Eph. 1:4). Nothing can alter or hinder what God has purposed from the beginning, and we are supported by that "eternal purpose" (Eph. 3:11).

+ **Jesus:** The foundation of all foundations is the Lord Himself. "For no one can lay another foundation than that which was laid, which is Jesus Christ" (1 Cor. 3:11). He is an infinite and "sure foundation" for all who call upon His name (Isa. 28:16 KJV).

Considering that you *have* such an everlasting foundation, it is fully believable that you can *be* an everlasting foundation on which God can build His work in this world. Regardless of how magnificent and lofty this calling may seem to be, dare to confess, "I am who God says I am."

DECLARE WHO YOU ARE IN CHRIST

I declare that I am called to be an everlasting foundation! As I serve God with stability, people around me will be able to build their hopes on the testimony of my life. I declare that the main reason I am an everlasting foundation is the fact that I have an everlasting foundation. God has undergirded me with an immovable and unchangeable base. My future is based and founded on God's imparted righteousness, the Word of God, the church of the living God, the apostles and prophets, the holy mountains, and on God's foundational plan. Most of all, the strongest foundation under me is the Lord Jesus Himself who has promised that He will never leave me nor forsake me. For this I am eternally grateful. In Jesus's name, amen!

Additional reading: Ezra 3:10–13; Job 4:18–19; Psalm 11:3 (NKJV); 2 Timothy 2:19; Revelation 17:8

Chapter 49

THE GENERAL ASSEMBLY AND CHURCH OF THE FIRSTBORN

But you have come to Mount Zion and to the city of the living God, the heavenly Jerusalem, and to an innumerable company of angels, to *the general assembly and church of the firstborn* who are enrolled in heaven; to God, the Judge of all; and to the spirits of the righteous ones made perfect.

—HEBREWS 12:22–23

EVERY NAME ASSIGNED to us in God's Word opens up a new area of revelation regarding who we are and what we possess as children of the Most High. This title appears only once in Scripture, yet provides one of the most powerful insights available concerning our spiritual identity, inheritance, and purpose.

The phrase "general assembly" communicates that this status is for every child of God. All who have gathered together under the headship of the Messiah are included—even those redeemed under the old covenant.[1]

The word *church* means called out ones, for God has "called" us "out of darkness into His marvelous light" (1 Pet. 2:9). He has called us out of spiritual depravity and destitution into righteousness, wholeness, and abundance. All who are washed in the blood of Jesus are equally loved, equally cleansed, equally righteous, and equally gifted with eternal life. For this reason, they are named the "church of the firstborn" (NKJV), or as another version states, "the whole Church in which everyone is a 'first-born son' and a citizen of heaven" (Heb. 12:23, JB).

THE FIRSTBORN STATUS

In the Hebrew culture being a firstborn son came with exceptional blessings, privileges, and responsibilities. The firstborn was the recipient of the birthright and the primary blessing. The birthright was the status of being the head of the household (following the demise of the father) and the primary inheritor of his estate. Though a blessing was normally given to all of the offspring, a greater, more potent blessing was reserved for the one occupying the firstborn status. (See Genesis 25:21–34; 27:1–41; 48:1–22; 49:1–33.)

A mystery of the kingdom of God unfolds when we inspect those who emerged as the "chosen ones," those occupying the firstborn son status, in the patriarchal line of the Old Testament:

+ Cain was literally Adam's firstborn, but went the way of evil. Abel was the second son, yet in a symbolic sense, he obtained the firstborn status, for his worship was received by God who supernaturally witnessed His approval. (See Genesis 4:1–2; Hebrews 11:4.)

+ Ishmael was literally Abraham's firstborn son by Hagar, but he was disinherited. Isaac was the second son by Sarah, a child of promise, and he obtained the firstborn status. (See Genesis 21:5–19.)

+ Esau was Isaac's literal firstborn son, but sold his birthright for a bowl of lentils. Jacob was the second son, beloved of God, and he obtained the firstborn status. (See Genesis 25:29–34; 27:1–41; Romans 9:13; Hebrews 12:16–17.)

+ Reuben was Jacob's literal firstborn son, but forfeited his inheritance because of sexual sin. Joseph was the eleventh son, yet he obtained the firstborn status and the coat of many colors. (See Genesis 37:1–11; 49:3–4.)

+ Manasseh was Joseph's literal firstborn son, but was passed over. Ephraim, the second son, obtained the firstborn status. (See Genesis 48:8–20.)

As you can see, over and over again, the first was last and the last was first—an evident spiritual pattern with God. (See Matthew 19:30; 20:16.) In these examples those qualified in the flesh to obtain the firstborn status never did obtain it, but those who were favored by God prevailed.

Even on a larger scale this pattern has persisted. Egypt was the greatest of all nations, but when God searched the world over to find a covenant people, He chose Israel, "the smallest of all nations" (Deut. 7:7, NLT). Thus, the least became the greatest, the lowest became the highest, the last became the first, and the "tail" became "the head" (Deut. 28:13). God even proclaimed, "Israel is My son, even My firstborn" (Exod. 4:22, KJV).

How does that relate to our membership in the "church of the firstborn"? None of us qualified by our own goodness or our own greatness to be included in God's family; we were saved by grace alone. Groveling in the guilt of our past, we were unfit for the kingdom of God, but God sent His unmerited love into our lives to lift us from the bottom to the top.

THE DOUBLE PORTION

In Hebrew tradition God decreed that the son occupying the "firstborn" status receive a "double portion" inheritance, which was also called "the right of the firstborn" (Deut. 21:17). This did not always mean twice as much; it just indicated a larger amount than all other distributions. The smaller remaining portion was divided among the other heirs.

Jesus was titled "the firstborn among many brothers" (Rom. 8:29), "the firstborn over all creation" (Col 1:15, NKJV), and "the firstborn from the dead" (Rev. 1:5). What was His double-portion inheritance? Could it be the dual aspect of His nature?

He was "the Word...made flesh" (John 1:14, KJV), and He had "the Spirit without measure" (John 3:34).

Amazingly these two things have been passed on to the church of the firstborn, for we have all been:

+ Begotten of the Word (See James 1:18, KJV; 1 Corinthians 4:15; 1 John 5:1.)

+ Born of the Spirit (John 3:1–7)

By these two inheritance gifts we are made whole for "of His fullness we have all received" (John 1:16, NKJV). Every child of God has this double-portion inheritance. Nothing can be added to it, for we are already "complete in Him" (Col. 2:10)!

In the resurrection these two aspects of our inheritance will be brought to utter perfection. We will also "inherit all things," in realms terrestrial and celestial (Rev. 21:7). So regardless of the disappointments and grief we have faced in this life, we can claim the prophetic promise God gave His people in Isaiah 61:7:

> Instead of your shame you shall have *double honor,* and instead of humiliation they shall rejoice over their portion. Therefore, in their land they shall possess *a double portion;* everlasting joy shall be theirs.

Although these truths are magnificent, the most wonderful promise is the fact that our names have been "enrolled in heaven" (Heb. 12:23). That is reason enough to shout God's praises for the rest of this earthly sojourn.

DECLARE WHO YOU ARE IN CHRIST

I declare that I belong to the church of the firstborn—the church in which every member is considered to be a firstborn son! The ground is level at the cross. I did not obtain this elite status by religious works or personal righteousness. It is a gift of grace. As a firstborn son, I have received a double-portion inheritance—being begotten of the Word and born of the Spirit. I am just as beloved of the Father as any other child of God, and nothing can be added to make me any more complete in Jesus. I have received of His fullness in Jesus's name, amen!

Additional reading: Isaiah 24:23; Obadiah 1:17–21; Micah 4:1–7; Philippians 3:20; Hebrews 12:1–25

Chapter 50

THE HEAVENLY

The first man is out of the earth, earthy; the second man is the Lord out of heaven; as is the earthy, such are also the earthy; and as is the heavenly, such are also the heavenly.
—1 Corinthians 15:47–48, ylt

BASICALLY THE ABOVE verses are saying that those who are unsaved are "of the earth" and can only receive earthly things in this life. They are motivated primarily by the five senses. Adam transferred that state of carnal limitation to all of us, physically and soulishly. But if we have a covenant connection to the Lord of heaven, all that He is and all that heaven can provide can pour into our lives as an inheritance right now.

We are not "the earthly"; we are "the heavenly."

Hebrews 3:1 also titles us "partakers of the heavenly calling" (kjv). That means four main things:

+ We have received a calling from heaven.
+ That calling will make us a conduit of heavenly things while we are on the earth.
+ That calling will lead us back to heaven at our departure from this world.
+ That calling will eventually bring us back with the Lord Jesus Christ when He descends from heaven and brings the kingdom of heaven fully to earth.

The two worlds were merged before the fall of Adam. The Garden of Eden was surely a "heaven-on-earth" atmosphere. Jesus showed us how that can happen again. In describing His own spiritual condition, He told Nicodemus: "No one has ascended to heaven except He who descended from heaven, even the Son of Man who is in heaven" (John 3:13).

Notice He claimed that even while walking on the earth, He was functioning in a heavenly sphere (hearing from the Father, being directed by the Spirit, and taking authority over demonic opposition and natural problems). You see Jesus didn't really come to set up another religion; He came to take us back to what Adam lost.

There are three main steps that will connect you this way to your "heavenly Father": repenting of your sin, acknowledging your need, and claiming your inheritance (Matt. 6:26).

REPENTING OF YOUR SIN

After Jesus came out of His time of temptation in the wilderness, His primary message was: "Repent! For the kingdom of heaven is at hand" (Matt. 4:17).

He was informing the people that heavenly influence and heavenly experiences were close to them, above them, all around them. God wanted heaven to break forth into their lives with its miraculous power. But they had to place themselves in a receptive position through sincere repentance (which includes genuine sorrow for sin, hatred for sin, departure from sin, and a sincere yielding to the will of God). When a person takes these steps, more is gained than lost. Instead of futilely trying to reach heaven by human effort (as they did at Babel), heaven comes down and reaches you.

ACKNOWLEDGING YOUR NEED

In His first main message to His disciples Jesus revealed: "Blessed are the poor in spirit! For theirs is the kingdom of heaven" (Matt. 5:3).

Notice this first beatitude does not say, "theirs *will be* the kingdom of heaven," but "theirs *is* the kingdom of heaven." So when you acknowledge your human, earthly lack, you can partake of heavenly abundance, right here, right now.

It's like tuning in to the radio. The waves are all around you, but they're invisible. First, someone has to convince you they exist (in a higher dimension, beyond your sensory range). Then someone has to give you the right equipment and show you how to turn on the knob. Then a whole new world opens up to you. The "knob" on this "heavenly radio" is poverty of spirit. When we turn our hearts toward God this way, we automatically tune in to a realm of wisdom, authority, creativity, and much more.

David is a great example of someone who showed poverty of spirit. Even though he was probably the wealthiest man of his day, he was not afraid to admit: "I am poor and needy; yet the LORD thinks about me" (Ps. 40:17).

Apparently no matter how much God promoted him, he always recognized his source and his complete dependency on the Lord. That's why heavenly things kept abounding in his life, even in tough times. We need to keep the same mind-set.

Claiming Your Inheritance

The last step in functioning as "the heavenly" involves seizing by faith what rightfully belongs to you. When you were born again, an incredible transition took place:

> But God, being rich in mercy, because of His great love with which He loved us, even when we were dead in sins, made us alive together with Christ (by grace you have been saved), and He raised us up and *seated us together in the heavenly places in Christ Jesus.*
>
> —Ephesians 2:4–6

So the moment you were spiritually reborn, the Spirit of God translated you into a heavenly position of authority, victory and rest in God. You are actually "seated with Christ" in heavenly places— not literally, but spiritually and figuratively. (See Revelation 3:21.) Your enemies are now your footstool (sin, the curse, all satanic plots). You occupy a position of supremacy now. But it gets even better. You should quote this verse out loud: "Blessed be the God and Father of our Lord Jesus Christ, who has blessed us with every spiritual blessing in the heavenly places in Christ" (Eph. 1:3).

Notice this promise in the past tense. God already has blessed us (we are already healed, already delivered, already joyous, already heirs of the wisdom and righteousness of God, already full of power and authority, already full of purpose and destiny). We just need to claim what rightfully belongs to us. One of the best ways of doing that is to speak the prayerful affirmation Jesus told us to pray: "Your kingdom come; Your will be done on earth, as it is in heaven" (Matt. 6:10).

So "in Christ" (in the Messiah) the two realms merge again. In a sense we can walk with God again, just as Adam did. We can function in the kingdom of heaven right now and partake of the kingdom of heaven right here, on our journey toward that incredible era when the kingdom of heaven will fully come to earth. John prophesied that glorious heavenly outcome:

> Then I saw "a new heaven and a new earth." For the first heaven and the first earth had passed away, and there was no more sea. I, John, saw the Holy City, the New Jerusalem, coming down out of heaven from God, prepared as a bride adorned for her husband. And I heard a loud voice from heaven, saying, "Look! The tabernacle of God is with men, and He will dwell with them. They shall be His people, and God Himself will be with them and be their God."
> —Revelation 21:1–3

Declare Who You Are in Christ

I declare that I am one of the heavenly! I claim my inheritance of being seated with Christ in heavenly places right now. I have ascended with the Lord Jesus, and I am enthroned with Him in a position of authority and victory, rest and supremacy. I am already blessed with all spiritual blessings in heavenly places in the Lord Jesus Christ. I am expecting an outpouring of heavenly wisdom, power, love, joy, and triumph in every earthly circumstance that I face. I am not bound to this earth and its limitations. I am an heir of unlimited heavenly resources. In Jesus's name, amen!

Additional reading: 1 Samuel 2:10; Malachi 3:10–12; Matthew 5:10–12; Revelation 22:1–21

Chapter 51

HEIRS OF THE KINGDOM

*Has God not chosen the poor of this world to
be rich in faith and heirs of the kingdom which
He promised to those who love Him?*
—JAMES 2:5

THE WORD KINGDOM simply means a king's domain. God's kingdom is that over which He rules: everything and everyone in heaven and earth, submitted to His authority, are part of His kingdom.

The terms "kingdom of God" and "kingdom of heaven" are synonymous, describing the same kingdom by referring to the One who rules over it or the place from which it is ruled.[1]

The concept of this spiritual kingdom and its advance in this world dominated Jesus's life and message:

+ After forty days of fasting, He came out of the wilderness preaching, "Repent! For the kingdom of heaven is at hand" (Matt. 4:17).

+ His first recorded sermon began with the statement, "Blessed are the poor in spirit, for theirs is the kingdom of heaven" (Matt. 5:3).

+ Many of His parables started with the phrase "the kingdom of heaven is like" (Matt. 13:24).

+ His message was called "the word of the kingdom" (Matt 13:19) and "the gospel of the kingdom" (Matt. 24:14).

+ After He rose from the dead, He spent forty days teaching His disciples things pertaining to "the kingdom of God" (Acts 1:3).

So from the beginning to the end of His earthly sojourn, the establishment of this spiritual kingdom was Jesus's all-consuming passion. When His disciples asked how they should pray, Jesus instructed them to say: "Our Father... Your kingdom come; Your will be done on earth, as it is in heaven" (Matt. 6:9–10).

Many thought this prayer would be answered in the manner of former God-sent deliverers in Israel—that the Messiah would raise up an army, banish the invaders, and restore the land to the Jews. But the strategy changed—dramatically. Jesus explained heaven's new battle plan by saying:

> The kingdom of God does not come with observation. Nor will they say, "Here it is!" or "There it is!" For remember, the kingdom of God is within you.
>
> —Luke 17:20–21

They didn't get it at first. They couldn't relate to this new thing that God was doing in the earth. But this divine kingdom was not going to proceed visibly by taking one blood-soaked battlefield after another. It was destined to instead advance invisibly, from one heart to another, as new converts were born again, absorbed into its citizenship, and filled with the love that permeates the kingdom. (See John 3:1–5; 17:26.)

This has been God's method for nearly two millennia. However, it's about to change drastically again. On the last day of this age the kingdom of God will take over the world fully in one blinding flash of glorious power. Jesus described that spectacular and visible event three verses later in Luke: "For as the lightning flashes and lights up the heavens from one side to the other, so will the Son of Man be in His day" (Luke 17:24).

Until that final climax happens, we are called to bring change to the world around us by manifesting kingdom character, kingdom power, and kingdom influence every single day.

WHAT THE KINGDOM "IS NOT"

In two key passages Paul explained what the kingdom of God is by telling us what it's not. Here is the first: "For the kingdom of God is not in word, but in power" (1 Cor. 4:20).

Theology is important. Doctrine is important. We need to be taught biblical principles. However, the main indication of living in the kingdom is not theological or intellectual; it's about the power of the Holy Spirit that brings transformation to people's hearts and lives. The Greek word translated "power" is *dunamis*, from which we get our word dynamite. That means the kingdom of God is an explosive idea! One moment of experiencing the power of God can accomplish more than two hundred hours of theological instruction or psychological counseling. Witnessing one actual healing or miracle is more powerful than attending an all-day seminar titled "How to Heal the Sick."

The second passage Paul uses is this: "For the kingdom of God is not eating and drinking, but righteousness and peace and joy in the Holy Spirit" (Rom. 14:17, NKJV).

Traditions can be important. Rituals and rules can make our spiritual lives predictable and stable. But we can also get stuck in the mud of religion. So the kingdom is not about "eating and drinking" (a reference to the dietary laws of the Old Testament); it's about being filled with the supernatural character of the King who rules the kingdom. It's much more important to experience a foretaste of the joy of heaven or flow in the love of God toward others than to keep all the biblical injunctions concerning proper food choices.

MIRACLES SHOULD BE THE NORM

When Jesus sent forth His seventy disciples, He told them to "preach, saying, 'The kingdom of heaven is at hand,'" but then He added: "Heal the sick, cleanse the lepers, raise the dead, and cast out demons. Freely you have received, freely give" (Matt. 10:7–8).

In other words Jesus was saying, "Tell them God can reign as a King in their lives. Tell them they can live in a spiritual kingdom. But then show them tangible proof of the practical and supernatural ways that kingdom living can be evidenced!" This is still the will of God for believers, for Jesus Christ is "the same yesterday, and today, and forever" (Heb. 13:8).

THE FINAL MANIFESTATION

One day the King of kings will not only heal sin-sick hearts and sick bodies, He will also bring total healing to a sick world system. When He returns in glory, the angel will declare: "The kingdoms of this world have become the kingdoms of our Lord, and of His Christ, and He shall reign forever and ever" (Rev. 11:15).

Our spiritual status will grow amazingly, for:

> The kingdom and dominion, and the greatness of all the kingdoms under the whole heaven, shall be given to the people of the saints of the Most High, whose kingdom is an everlasting kingdom, and all dominions shall serve and obey Him.
> —DANIEL 7:27

So being "heirs of the kingdom" is both a present and future inheritance. Our desire should be to spiritually abide in God's kingdom right now, manifesting its character and permeating society with its values. But our continual hope should be to reign with the Messiah in that fully manifested kingdom which is yet to come. As we journey that direction, we can be assured, in all the unpredictable battles we face in life, that His "kingdom...cannot be shaken" (Heb. 12:28, NKJV)!

Therefore, the same is true of us.

DECLARE WHO YOU ARE IN CHRIST

I declare that I am an heir of the kingdom! I have inherited the nature and the authority of the eternal King. His kingdom love is stronger than any bitterness I face. His kingdom joy is greater than any depression that weighs me down. His kingdom peace is more stabilizing than any anxiety that temporarily overwhelms me. When I was born again, I was translated into the kingdom of God. Now I claim its daily manifestation in my life by prayerfully affirming, "Father, Your kingdom come, Your will be done on earth, as it is in heaven." In Jesus's name, amen!

Additional reading: Psalm 145:10–13; Isaiah 9:6–7; Matthew 13:1–11; John 3:1–5; Colossians 1:13

Chapter 52

THE PILLAR AND FOUNDATION OF THE TRUTH

But if I am delayed, you might know how you ought to
conduct yourself in the house of God, which is the church
of the living God, *the pillar and foundation of truth.*
—1 TIMOTHY 3:15

AN EXPERTLY AND artistically fashioned pillar can speak to our
hearts in a number of symbolic ways—representing qualities
such as uprightness, authority, strength, stability, dominion, greatness, excellence, and permanence.

Towering, ornately designed columns can also denote that which
is exalted, admirable, praiseworthy, awe-inspiring, and superior—
words that embody the highest ideals of men and women who desire
to achieve their maximum, God-given potential.

Such devoted, pillar-like individuals are especially needed when
the selfish side of human nature dominates a culture or an era, when
people become far too violent, lustful, greedy, and blasphemous,
when the sacred is lightly esteemed or even scorned and profaned. In
such "perilous times" heaven ordains choice men and women to courageously lay the foundation of truth once again and rear up a pillar-
like standard to turn back the hearts of the wayward (2 Tim. 3:1).

It was such a time of national crisis when God called Jeremiah.
Though the prophet insisted that his youthfulness disqualified him,
the Lord countered:

> "For you shall go to all to whom I send you, and whatever I
> command you, you shall speak. Do not be afraid of their
> faces....For behold, I have made you this day a fortified
> city and an iron pillar, and bronze walls against the whole
> land....They will fight against you, but they shall not prevail
> against you. For I am with you," says the LORD, "to deliver you."
> —JEREMIAH 1:7–8, 18–19, NKJV

God made Jeremiah, the boy prophet, an "iron pillar"—an unbending, unchanging, uncompromising voice of prophetic truth—a memorial of righteousness that God's people would look back to for many centuries to come.

PILLARS OF THE EARTH

Hannah, the mother of Samuel, revealed this calling on all of God's people in a very beautiful and poetical way—declaring of God that:

> He raises the poor from the dust and lifts the beggar from the ash heap, to set them among princes and make them inherit the throne of glory. For *the pillars of the earth* are the LORD's, and He has set the world upon them.
>
> —1 SAMUEL 2:8, NKJV

As we covered in an earlier chapter titled "Kings," the beginning of this unique verse speaks of the transformation that comes to those who covenant with God:

+ *"He raises the poor from the dust."* He elevates those who are "poor in spirit" from the "dust" of their own mortality—the bondage of a mere, temporal, fleshly existence (Matt. 5:3).
+ *"He lifts the beggar from the dunghill and the ash heap."* (The King James Version translates "ash heap" as "dunghill.") He delivers those who plead for mercy from the "dunghill" of carnality—a sensual, base, egocentric lifestyle—and the "ash heap" of the destroyed life that results.

Once they are loosed, God positions the repentant among princes—adopting them into a royal lineage. They become sons and daughters of the great King, destined to reign with Him forever. So God intends to dramatically lift His people from the dust of insignificance.

Those chosen for such a destiny also become "pillars of the earth," not only in the future kingdom of God, but also right here, right now. The world rests upon them—for they often become significant players and major influencers in shaping society. They become God's catalyst for change, His means of introducing kingdom values in a world quite opposed to them.

Grand evidence of this can be found in the Puritans. Their prayerful, covenant community at Plymouth Rock evolved through the centuries into a democratic republic that has since spread its influence worldwide: politically, governmentally, religiously, and spiritually. Though most of them were humble and unassuming, mere farmers and fishermen—in reality they were "pillars of the earth," raised high above the human race, a means of impacting the world with kingdom values. God still needs choice individuals like this.

PILLARS FROM THE PAST

Peter, James, and John were considered "pillars" in the early Jerusalem church—for they boldly supported the claim that Yeshua (Jesus) was truly the Messiah and that He rose from the dead. (See Galatians 2:9.) Faithful unto death themselves, they refused to be deterred.

About fifteen hundred years later a God-fearing Catholic monk named Martin Luther emerged as a "pillar" of the Reformation—declaring that "the just shall live by faith," not by allegiance to an organization or participation in church rituals and traditions (Rom. 1:17). He refused to be intimidated, though church authorities threatened to burn him at the stake.

About four hundred years into the future his namesake, Martin Luther King, emerged as a "pillar" in the civil rights movement and was used of God to champion equality and justice for all races. His memory and influence have lived on, though he suffered a tragic, untimely death.

And thousands of others could be mentioned, stretching across two thousand years of church history—all common believers who showed uncommon commitment to God. They were ordinary men and women who were used by God in extraordinary ways. Like Jakin and Boaz (the two, imposing, thirty-five-foot-high pillars that flanked the entrance to the temple of Solomon) these pillar-like believers have guided multitudes into the presence of God through their testimonies. (See 1 Kings 7:21; 2 Chronicles 3:17.)[1]

PILLARS OF TRUTH

In our theme scripture Paul declared that the church is called to be "the pillar and foundation of the truth" (1 Tim. 3:15). What a challenge in a world so prone to duplicity and hypocrisy! Other translations call God's people "the pillar and support of the truth" (CJB) or "the pillar and bulwark of the truth" (EMTV).

A foundation is the base on which something is built. A pillar can be a supporting column in a building or one that stands by itself as a memorial. A bulwark is a rampart or wall of dirt or some other material reared up as a defense. All three images speak a powerful message concerning the important role of the church, especially in these last days.

The entire earth is saturated with deception. Satan is even referred to as the "great dragon" who "deceives the whole world" (Rev. 12:9). But the church is a memorial "pillar" raised up high above all nations, radiating the bright light of truth. The church is also a mighty "bulwark," an unconquerable barrier raised up against the onslaught of lies that besiege the hearts and minds of human beings.

We are well equipped for this *monumental* task, for the "God of truth" (Deut. 32:4, NKJV) has given us "the word of truth" (Eph. 1:13) and filled us with "the Spirit of truth" to "guide" us "into all truth" (John 16:13). As we "walk in truth" (3 John 1:4), the One who said "I am...the truth" (John 14:6) will show us how to take a pillar-like stand. When Pilate asked Him, "Are you a king?" the Messiah responded: "For this cause I was born, and for this cause I have come into the world, that I should bear witness to the truth" (John 18:37, NKJV).

What Jesus said that day we should boldly echo, for we too have been called to "bear witness to the truth."

PILLARS IN GOD'S TEMPLE ETERNALLY

If we faithfully fulfill our charge in this world, there will be a great day of reward in the world to come. God has already promised:

> He who overcomes will I make him *a pillar in the temple of My God*, and he shall go out no more. I will write on him the name of My God and the name of the city of My God, the

New Jerusalem, which comes down out of heaven from My
God, and My own new name.

—Revelation 3:12

As supporting pillars in God's eternal temple, we will be the
infrastructure of God's government established unshakably in
heaven and on earth. As king-priests reigning with Him, we will
uphold God's standards with a rod of iron throughout the glorious
new creation—a vast kingdom represented as a singular temple, for
everything and everyone will be immersed in the worshipful atmosphere that will emanate universally from the King of all kings.

We await with awe-filled hearts until God turns the page to the
last chapter in this amazing book that He is writing.

Declare Who You Are in Christ

*I declare that I am part of the pillar and foundation of the
truth! Therefore I make a quality decision—I will embrace
the truth, love the truth, live the truth, and declare the truth
to my generation. I am determined to be like a pillar—
strong, uncompromising, honorable, steadfast, and stable—
in the midst of a weak, confused, and unstable world. I
recognize that God has raised me from the dust, the dunghill, and the ash heap to fulfill this calling, so I give Him
all the glory for any good I will ever accomplish. In Jesus's
name, amen!*

Additional reading: Genesis 28:10–22; 31:1–55; Exodus 24:1–4;
Psalm 144:12 (NKJV), Proverbs 9:1; Revelation 10:1

CONCLUSION

WHEN I WAS a boy I often explored the woods near my home, collecting cocoons during the early spring. Then I would tape them to the walls of my bedroom. (God bless my mother for her patience and kindness!) A few weeks later, with sheer joy, I would watch as gorgeous, multicolored butterflies and moths emerged from temporary lifeless shells (pupas) to seize their real identity (an amazing process called metamorphosis).

I never grew bored watching those delicate and beautiful creatures ready themselves for flight, perched on my forefinger or on the posts of my bed. Very slowly they moved their new wings up and down—over and over again—to strengthen themselves before attempting something they had never done before. I normally interacted with them for a day or two. Then with mixed emotions I would take them outside to release them into their natural habitat—so they could fully enjoy their brief existence, doing what they were created to do and being what they were created to be.

Though I don't collect cocoons anymore, to this day I am still awed by what I witnessed. On a much higher level, though, I am constantly involved in observing a similar process. As a teacher of God's Word, one of my greatest joys is watching people come out of their spiritual cocoons. I love helping ordinary Christians become extraordinary champions for the kingdom of God. Often the thing that triggers such an awakening is the self-discovery that results from encountering this amazing and vital message God has given me for His people—finding out who we are in God's great plan and then boldly walking in our new identity.

THE TRANSITION FROM THINKING TO DOING

There is a Greek word in the New Testament that fits very appropriately in this epilogue: *metamorphoo* (pronounced met-am-or-fo'-o).

Go ahead. Try and pronounce that one out loud, especially if no one is near enough to hear.

Metamorphoo appears only four times in the New Testament and you probably guessed it—it's the word from which we derive our English term *metamorphosis*.

Look up that word in the dictionary and you'll find some powerful definitions:

+ "A profound change in form from one stage to the next in the life history of an organism."
+ "Any complete change in appearance, character, or circumstances."[1]

I am expecting a supernatural metamorphosis for you—a "profound change" in your life history, and a "complete change" in your character and the circumstances of your life (and one day, at the Lord's return, a complete change in appearance as well).

Every great accomplishment or change usually happens twice. First, it takes place in the mind, in thought form, and then it happens in reality. The Bible verifies that by the way the word *metamorphoo* is used.

First, a *metamorphosis* has to happen in our thinking—in the way we view ourselves and our relationships—both with God and with others. Concerning this mind-set development, Paul, exhorts:

> Do not be conformed to this world, but be *transformed* by the renewing of your mind, that you may prove what is that good and acceptable and perfect will of God.
>
> —ROMANS 12:2

The word "transformed" is translated from the Greek *metamorphoo*.

The will of God for you is not just about what you shouldn't do (all the "Thou shalt nots!"). More importantly it's about what you should do and what you have the potential of becoming—your gifts, your purpose, and your destiny. It's the deep calling to the deep—God's *deep* longing to see you fulfill your sonship purpose and your *deep* longing to successfully achieve that goal (Ps. 42:7).

Hopefully absorbing this revelation of *Who Am I?* has helped to awaken such a mental metamorphosis in you. Surely by now, you often spend prayerful moments pondering the deeper aspects of who you are and what you can accomplish in this world. But that's just the beginning of the process.

Now you need to proceed from step 1 (thinking) to step 2 (doing). That's a far more important phase in God's agenda for you. Here's a powerful passage describing that kind of transition:

> But we all, with unveiled face, beholding as in a mirror the glory of the Lord, are being *transformed* into the same image from glory to glory, just as by the Spirit of the Lord.
> —2 Corinthians 3:18, nkjv

The word *transformed* is once again translated from the Greek *metamorphoo*.

This verse is not just about being changed in the way you think (your self-image); it's about a new you manifesting, the power of truly becoming a world changer and history maker in both practical and radical ways. When you see Jesus in all of His glory—reflected in the "mirror" of the Word of God—automatically it should cause a replication in you of a similar earthly purpose (James 1:23). The Scripture teaches that the everlasting Father has chosen you from the beginning, and that you have been "predestined to be conformed to the image of His Son, that He might be the firstborn among many brethren" (Rom. 8:29).

So this is far bigger than your human will; it's part of the everlasting plan of God that you follow the firstborn Son and imitate His ways. Once this dominates your mind-set as a Christian, get ready for a remarkable *metamorphosis* in the way you function on a day-to-day basis. Yes, get ready to ascend "from glory to glory"—from the *glorious* change that has already happened inwardly, to the *glorious* things God will do through you outwardly.

Hopefully as soon as you absorbed the introduction of this book, you were already pushing through the walls of your spiritual cocoon, and with each succeeding chapter you have continued pressing against the constraints, more and more, until you have broken free completely.

Now it's time to perch on God's forefinger, flex your wings, and get ready to attempt some things you've never done before. Yes, it's time—time to soar into your God-given destiny, time to become who God says you are.

Go ahead, spread your wings. Take a leap of faith into the unknown.

The breath of God will be the wind beneath your wings. And He knows exactly where you need to go in the next stage of this spiritual quest.

Let me know what happens. I'm very interested. I may not know you by name, but you are very important to God and to me as well.

I might just tape your testimony on one of the walls of my office.

NOTES

Chapter 2—His Beloved

1. Matthew Henry, *Henry Commentary on the Whole Bible*, s. v. "Hosea," accessed March 1, 2016, Bible Study Tools, http://www.biblestudytools.com /commentaries/matthew-henry-complete/hosea/1.html. Matthew Henry offers that Jezreel means the scattered of God. *The Pulpit Commentary* agrees, sharing that in the Hebrew, the word for Jezreel (*Yisreel*) is very similar to Israel (*Yisrael*). This similarity was intentionally used to make the prophetic connection all the more profound—the declaration that *Yisrael*, the prince of God, was soon to be *Yisreel*, the scattered of God.

2. William Smith, *Smith's Bible Dictionary*, s.v. "Ammi," Bible Study Tools, accessed March 1, 2016, http://www.biblestudytools.com/dictionaries /smiths-bible-dictionary/ammi.html; Smith, *Smith's Bible Dictionary*, s.v. "Ruhamah," Bible Study Tools, accessed March 1, 2016, http://www.bible studytools.com/dictionaries/smiths-bible-dictionary/ruhamah.html.

3. Smith, *Smith's Bible Dictionary*, s.v. "Jezreel," Biblestudytools.com, accessed March 1, 2016, 2016, http://www.biblestudytools.com/dictionaries /smiths-bible-dictionary/jezre-el.html.

Chapter 3—The Bride

1. "Jerusalem," International Standard Bible Encyclopedia Online, accessed March 1, 2016, http://www.internationalstandardbible.com/J/jerusalem-1.html.

Chapter 4—Children of Promise

1. Herbert Lockyer, *All the Promises of the Bible* (Grand Rapids, MI: Lamplighter Books, Zondervan Publishing Company, 1962), 10.

Chapter 6—Heirs of the Grace of Life

1. James Strong, *Strong's Exhaustive Concordance*, s.v. "grace," BibleHub.com, accessed May 4, 2016, http://biblehub.com/greek/5485.htm.

Chapter 8—The Blessed of the Father

1. See chapter 17, "The Poor in Spirit."

Chapter 9—The Body of Christ

1. "Abraham Lincoln Quotes," AZQuotes, accessed February 8, 2016, http:// www.azquotes.com/quote/809154.

2. "Augustine of Hippo Quotes," GoodReads.com, accessed March 14, 2016, http://www.goodreads.com/quotes/332507-in-essentials-unity-in-non-essentials -liberty-in-all-things-charity.

Chapter 11—An Inheritor of His Mountains

1. But we have certainly not replaced Israel. The "Israel of God" is an eternal institution ultimately made up of those truly redeemed under both covenants (Gal. 6:16).

Chapter 12—The Just

1. Roland H. Bainton, Here I Stand, A Life of Martin Luther (Nashville: Abington Press, 1978), 49.

Chapter 14—The Temple of God

1. Alfred Edersheim, *The Temple: Its Ministry and Services* (Peabody, MA: Hendrickson Publishers, 1994), 140–141; Kevin J. Conner, *The Temple of Solomon* (Blackburn, Victoria, Australia: Acacia Press Pty, LTD, 1988), 144.

2. Finis Jennings Dake, *Dake's Annotated Reference Bible* (Lawrenceville, GA; Dake Bible Sales), 454

3. The last two additional readings in the Book of the Revelation describe "heavenly furniture" (menorah lampstands and a golden incense altar) that perfectly match "earthly furniture" in the Temple of Solomon. Apparently the earthly was actually made after the pattern of the heavenly. (See Hebrews 8:4–5; 9:23–24.)

Chapter 16—A New Creation

1. "Anothen," Thayer's and Smith's Bible Dictionary, Biblestudytools.com, accessed March 14, 2016, http://www.biblestudytools.com/lexicons/greek/kjv/anothen.html.

Chapter 19—Saints

1. Strong, *Strong's Exhaustive Concordance*, s.v. "ekklésia," BibleHub.com, accessed May 4, 2016, http://biblehub.com/greek/1577.htm.

2. Walter A. Elwell, *Evangelical Dictionary of Theology*, s.v. "sanctification," Biblestudytools.com, accessed March 14, 2016, http://www.biblestudytools.com/dictionaries/bakers-evangelical-dictionary/sanctification.html.

Chapter 23—The Church

1. After His crucifixion, Jesus went down into "the lower parts of the earth" (Eph 4:9) and "the gospel was preached" to those who were dead (1 Pet. 4:6). Apparently at that point all Israelites redeemed under the old covenant were "called out" in a final sense, given an opportunity to receive Jesus as their true Messiah, loosed from the final vestige of death's power, and welcomed into the third heaven. In an eternal sense that's when they fully joined the ranks of this eternal institution called the church.

2. This title for God's people is explained in the last chapter of this book under the heading, "Pillars of the Earth."

CHAPTER 24—THE CONTRITE ONES

1. Albert M. Wells, *Inspiring Quotations, Contemporary and Classical* (Nashville: Thomas Nelson Publishers, 1988), 171, #2266.

2. Thomas á Kempis, *The Inner Life* trans. Leo Sherley-Price (New York: Penguin Group, 2005).

3. Erwin W. Lutzer, "Totally Yielded to God," Moody Church Media, accessed March 14, 2016, http://www.moodymedia.org/articles/moody-man-our -times/.

4. Ibid.

CHAPTER 25—DISCIPLES

1. Found at BibleGateway.com

2. Strong's, *Strong's Exhaustive Concordance*, s.v. "*miseó*," BibleHub.com, accessed May 4, 2016, http://biblehub.com/greek/3404.htm.

3. Dake, *Dake's Annotated Reference Bible*, 313–316.

4. Strong's, *Strong's Exhaustive Concordance*, s.v. "exousia," BibleHub.com, accessed May 4, 2016, http://biblehub.com/greek/1849.htm.

5. Strong's, *Strong's Exhaustive Concordance*, s.v. "dunamis," BibleHub.com, accessed May 4, 2016, http://biblehub.com/greek/1411.htm.

6. Matthew George Easton, *Easton's Bible Dictionary*, s.v. "Beelzebub," Biblestudytools.com, accessed March 14, 2016, http://www.biblestudytools.com /dictionaries/eastons-bible-dictionary/beelzebub.html.

CHAPTER 28—THE SALT OF THE EARTH

1. "Theodore Roosevelt Quotes," Brainy Quote, March 14, 2016, http://www .brainyquote.com/quotes/quotes/t/theodorero122742.html.

2. "Worth Your Salt," Idiom Origins, accessed March 14, 2016, http://idiom origins.net/worth-your-salt/.

CHAPTER 29—TRUE WORSHIPPERS

1. "Jesus, Thou Everlasting King" by Isaac Watts. Public domain.

CHAPTER 31—HIS ANOINTED

1. Strong's, *Strong's Exhaustive Concordance*, s.v. "*mashiyach*" BibleHub.com, accessed May 4, 2016, http://biblehub.com/greek/3323.htm; Herbert Lockyer, *All the Divine Names and Titles in the Bible* (Grand Rapids, MI: Zondervan Publishing House, 1975), 206.

CHAPTER 34—THE HOUSEHOLD OF FAITH

1. William Booth, "The Founder's Message to Soldiers," *Christianity Today*, October 5, 1992, 48.

CHAPTER 35—ORACLES OF GOD

1. This is actually a Hebrew idiom that means prohibiting and permitting—in other words, setting standards of moral behavior. The Complete Jewish Bible

says, "Whatever you prohibit on earth will be prohibited in heaven, and whatever you permit on earth will be permitted in heaven." However, it still shows an enormous amount of authority that God acknowledges.

CHAPTER 37—WITNESSES

1. Strong, *Strong's Exhaustive Concordance*, s.v. *"suneidésis,"* BibleHub.com, accessed May 4, 2016, http://biblehub.com/greek/4893.htm.
2. Strong, *Strong's Exhaustive Concordance*, s.v. *"dunamis."*

CHAPTER 38—THE HEAD

1. "The History of Ancient Palestine From the Early Bronze Age to the Roman Empire, Including the Coming of the Israelites, the Kingdom of David and Solomon, the Exile and the Destruction of the Temple," TimeMaps, accessed March 15, 2016, http://www.timemaps.com/history-of-ancient -palestine#maccabbees.

CHAPTER 39—HEIRS OF GOD

1. Most of these titles have been included in this book and explained individually.

CHAPTER 40—HEIRS OF SALVATION

1. "Isaiah, 1–7," International Standard Bible Encyclopedia Online, accessed February 22, 2016, http://www.internationalstandardbible.com/I/isaiah-1-7.html.
2. "Sozo," Thayer's and Smith's Bible Dictionary, Bible Study Tools, accessed March 14, 2016, http://www.biblestudytools.com/lexicons/greek/kjv/sozo.html.

CHAPTER 42—KINGS

1. To learn more about the grace of God and how God transfers a righteous status to His people, read the chapters titled "Heirs of the Grace of Life" and "The Just."

CHAPTER 43—MORE THAN CONQUERORS

1. It is very encouraging and edifying to go through the entire Bible and study every Holy Spirit-inspired prayer for the people of God and accept it as a petition the Father has already answered and poured out on you, such as Psalm 20:1–5, Romans 15:5–6, Ephesians 1:15–23, 1 Thessalonians 5:23; and Hebrews 13:20–21.

CHAPTER 45—CHILDREN OF THE RESURRECTION

1. Strong, *Strong's Exhaustive Concordance*, s.v. *"anastasis,"* BibleHub.com, accessed May 4, 2016, http://biblehub.com/greek/386.htm.

CHAPTER 46—CHILDREN OF ZION

1. Paul J. Achtemeier, *Harper's Bible Dictionary* (San Francisco: Harper & Row Publishers, 1985), 1165, s.v. "Zion."

Chapter 47—A Chosen Generation

1. Russky Pastyr, "'The Church of Christ Shall Not Be Impoverished' Sermon on the feast day of Apostle Matthias," accessed March 17, 2016, http://www .russianorthodoxchurch.ws/01newstucture/pagesen/sermons/stjohnmathias.html

Chapter 49—The General Assembly and Church of the Firstborn

1. It would be beneficial to study chapter 23, "The Church," for foundational information even before examining the revelation in this chapter. For instance, the mystery is explained how Old Testament redeemed persons, in a sense, became a part of "the church" when they responded to Jesus's preaching in Abraham's Bosom after His death on Calvary.

Chapter 51—Heirs of the Kingdom

1. The term "kingdom of heaven" is found exclusively in the Gospel of Matthew. However, parallel passages in the other Gospels use the term "kingdom of God," showing that these two ways of describing God's kingdom are interchangeable.

Chapter 52—The Pillar and Foundation of the Truth

1. *Jakin* means "God will establish," and *Boaz* means "in Him is strength." If we are consecrated new covenant temples of God, these two pillar-like attitudes should be reared at the gateway to our hearts and lives. Definitions cited from Dake, *Dake's Annotated Reference Bible*, 454.

Conclusion

1. "Metamorphosis," Dictionary.com, accessed March 17, 2016, http:// dictionary.reference.com/browse/metamorphosis?s=.

ABOUT THE AUTHOR

MIKE SHREVE was saved in 1970 during the Jesus movement era. He was a teacher of yoga at four Florida universities until an encounter with Jesus changed everything. His conversion story is featured in several books: *In Search of the True Light* (a comparison of over twenty religions), *Truth Seekers* (co-written with Sid Roth), and a mini-book called *The Highest Adventure: Encountering God* (offered as a free download on his websites).

Shortly after receiving salvation, Shreve began traveling evangelistically, preaching in hundreds of churches and conducting large open air crusades in various nations, such as India, Costa Rica, Liberia and Nigeria. He and his wife, Elizabeth, presently pastor an interdenominational church in Cleveland, Tennessee, called The Sanctuary.

Around 1985, Shreve began researching the names and titles God has given His offspring in Scripture. Discovering over one thousand, he realized he had found a mother lode of gold in God's Word. This resulted in a detailed, eight-volume series called *Our Glorious Inheritance, the Revelation of the Titles of the Children of God.* This new offering named *Who Am I?* is a compilation of fifty-two of the most profound titles drawn from the previous study. Weekly video teachings are offered online on this subject through Deeper Revelation International School of Ministry.

Shreve holds a bachelor of theology degree from Christian Life School of Theology and an honorary doctorate from Faith Theological Seminary in Tampa, Florida. He and Elizabeth believe in living a life of faith, joy and compassion, making every day an act of worship. They have two children: Zion Seth and Destiny Hope.

Volume four of the eight-volume series

 /mrshreve   @mike_shreve  mikeshreve@shreveministries.org

www.shreveministries.org / www.thetruelight.net / www.deeperrevelationbooks.org

P.O. Box 4260, Cleveland, TN 37320 / Office phone: 423-478-2843

CONNECT WITH US!

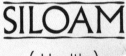